THE STRUCTURE OF
COMPETITIVE INDUSTRY

THE CAMBRIDGE ECONOMIC HANDBOOKS

General Editors

J. M. KEYNES (Lord Keynes)	1922–1936
D. H. ROBERTSON (Sir Dennis Robertson)	1936–1946
C. W. GUILLEBAUD	1946–1956
C. W. GUILLEBAUD ⎫ MILTON FRIEDMAN ⎭	1956–

THE STRUCTURE OF COMPETITIVE INDUSTRY

E. A. G. ROBINSON

M.A., F.B.A.

Fellow of Sidney Sussex College, Cambridge
Professor of Economics in the University of Cambridge

DIGSWELL PLACE
JAMES NISBET & CO. LTD.
CAMBRIDGE
AT THE UNIVERSITY PRESS

First published *1931*
Revised . . . . *January 1935*
Reprinted *1937*
　　　　1940, 1941, 1943, 1945 twice,
　　　　　1946, 1947, 1948, 1950
Revised *1953*
Reprinted *1953, 1956*
Revised and Reset . . . . *October 1958*
Reprinted *1959, 1960, 1964*

James Nisbet and Company, Limited
Digswell Place, Welwyn, Herts,
and the Cambridge University Press
in association with the University of Chicago Press

26,884

INTRODUCTION

TO THE CAMBRIDGE ECONOMIC HANDBOOKS
BY THE GENERAL EDITORS

Soon after the war of 1914–18 there seemed to be a place for a series of short introductory handbooks, 'intended to convey to the ordinary reader and to the uninitiated student some conception of the general principles of thought which economists now apply to economic problems'.

This Series was planned and edited by the late Lord Keynes under the title 'Cambridge Economic Handbooks' and he wrote for it a General Editorial Introduction of which the words quoted above formed part. In 1936 Keynes handed over the editorship of the Series to Mr. D. H. Robertson, who held it till 1946, when he was succeeded by Mr. C. W. Guillebaud.

It was symptomatic of the changes which had been taking place in the inter-war period in the development of economics, changes associated in a considerable measure with the work and influence of Keynes himself, that within a few years the text of part of the Editorial Introduction should have needed revision. In its original version the last paragraph of the Introduction ran as follows:

'Even on matters of principle there is not yet a complete unanimity of opinion amongst professional economists. Generally speaking, the writers of these volumes believe themselves to be orthodox members of the Cambridge School of Economics. At any rate, most of their ideas about the subject, and even their prejudices, are traceable to the contact they have enjoyed with the writings and lectures of the two economists who have chiefly influenced

Cambridge thought for the past fifty years, Dr. Marshall and Professor Pigou.'

Keynes later amended this concluding paragraph to read:

'Even on matters of principle there is not yet a complete unanimity of opinion amongst professional students of the subject. Immediately after the war (of 1914–18) daily economic events were of such a startling character as to divert attention from theoretical complexities. But today, economic science has recovered its wind. Traditional treatments and traditional solutions are being questioned, improved and revised. In the end this activity of research should clear up controversy. But for the moment controversy and doubt are increased. The writers of this Series must apologize to the general reader and to the beginner if many parts of their subject have not yet reached to a degree of certainty and lucidity which would make them easy and straightforward reading.'

Many though by no means all the controversies which Keynes had in mind when he penned these words have since been resolved. The new ideas and new criticisms, which then seemed to threaten to overturn the old orthodoxy, have, in the outcome, been absorbed within it and have served rather to strengthen and deepen it, by adding needed modifications and changing emphasis, and by introducing an altered and on the whole more precise terminology. The undergrowth which for a time concealed that main stream of economic thought to which Keynes referred in his initial comment and to which he contributed so greatly has by now been largely cleared away so that there is again a large measure of agreement among economists of all countries on the fundamental theoretical aspects of their subject.

This agreement on economic analysis is accompanied by wide divergence of views on questions of economic policy. These reflect both different estimates of the quantitative importance of one or another of the conflicting forces involved in any prediction about the consequences of a policy measure and different value judgments about the desirability of the predicted outcome. It still remains as true to-day as it was when Keynes wrote that—to quote once more from his Introduction:

'The Theory of Economics does not furnish a body of settled conclusions immediately applicable to policy. It is a method rather than a doctrine, an apparatus of the mind, a technique of thinking, which helps its possessor to draw correct conclusions.'

This method, while in one sense eternally the same, is in another ever changing. It is continually being applied to new problems raised by the continual shifts in policy views. This is reflected in the wide range of topics covered by the Cambridge Economic Handbooks already published, and in the continual emergence of new topics demanding coverage. Such a series as this should accordingly itself be a living entity, growing and adapting to the changing interests of the times, rather than a fixed number of essays on a set plan.

The wide welcome given to the Series has amply justified the judgment of its founder. Apart from its circulation in the British Empire, it has been published from the start in the United States of America, and translations of the principal volumes have appeared in a number of foreign languages.

The present change to joint Anglo-American editorship is designed to increase still further the usefulness of the Series by expanding the range of potential topics, authors and readers alike. It will succeed in its aim if it enables us to bring to a wide audience on both sides of the Atlantic lucid explanations and significant applications of 'that technique of thinking' which is the hallmark of economics as a science.

April 1957   C. W. GUILLEBAUD
                                         MILTON FRIEDMAN

CONTENTS

CHAPTER I

INTRODUCTORY

§ 1.   The Meaning of Industrial Efficiency .   .   1
§ 2.   Some Difficulties of Definition   3

CHAPTER II

THE OPTIMUM FIRM

§ 1.   The Concept of the Optimum Firm .   .   .   10
§ 2.   The Division of Labour and the Size of the
       Optimum Technical Unit   13
§ 3.   The Integration of Processes   19
§ 4.   Vertical Disintegration   19
§ 5.   The Economy of the Large Machine   .   .   20
§ 6.   The Balance of Processes.   25
§ 7.   Economies of Massed Reserves   .   .   .   26
§ 8.   Economies through the Large Organisation   .   27
§ 9.   Economies through Standardisation .   .   .   28
§ 10. The Trend of Size   30
§ 11. The Relation of the Optimum Technical Unit to
       the Optimum Firm   31

CHAPTER III

THE OPTIMUM MANAGERIAL UNIT

§ 1.   Managerial Division of Labour   .   .   .   34
§ 2.   Further Economies of Large Managements   .   37
§ 3.   The Limits to the Gains of Large Management .   39

§ 4. The Problem of Co-ordination . . . 40
§ 5. The Advantages of Small Managements . . 43
§ 6. The Importance of Individuals 45
§ 7. Does Management Set a Limit? . . . 46

CHAPTER IV

THE OPTIMUM FINANCIAL UNIT

§ 1. The Borrowing Powers of Firms . . . 50
§ 2. Methods and Rates of Growth. . . . 51
§ 3. The Influence of Forms of Organisation upon
      Enterprise 53
§ 4. The Advantages of the Large Financial Unit . 56
§ 5. Does Finance Set a Limit? 57

CHAPTER V

THE OPTIMUM MARKETING UNIT

§ 1. The Scope of Marketing Efficiency . . . 59
§ 2. The Economies of Large Scale Buying . . 60
§ 3. Sales Costs and a Difficulty of Analysis . . 62
§ 4. The Economies of Large Scale Selling . . 64
§ 5. Vertical Disintegration in Selling . . . 65
§ 6. Common Marketing Economies . . . 68
§ 7. Marketing Costs and the Optimum Firm . . 70

CHAPTER VI

THE INFLUENCE OF RISKS AND FLUCTUATIONS

§ 1. The Effects of Risk and Fluctuations . . 74
§ 2. Permanent Changes of Demand . . . 74
§ 3. Cyclical Variations of Demand . . . 77
§ 4. A Digression on Short Period Price . . . 78
§ 5. The Readjustment of Industry . . . 79

§ 6. The Effects of Curtailment of Output on Efficiency
and Survival 81
§ 7. Seasonal Variations of Demand . . . 85
§ 8. Erratic Variations of Demand 87
§ 9. Combination and Risk 88
§ 10. Technical Progress and Risk 91
§ 11. Spreading Risks 92

CHAPTER VII

THE RECONCILIATION OF DIFFERING OPTIMA

§ 1. The Problem of Reconciliation. . . . 94
§ 2. Vertical Disintegration 96
§ 3. Further Devices for Reconciliation . . . 99

CHAPTER VIII

THE PROBLEM OF GROWTH

§ 1. The Cost of Growth 104
§ 2. The Discontinuity of Increases of Efficiency . 105
§ 3. Expansion and Combination 107
§ 4. Types of Vertical Integration 110
§ 5. Lateral Integration 114
§ 6. The Multi-Product Firm 116

CHAPTER IX

THE OPTIMUM INDUSTRY

§ 1. The Relation of Cost to the Scale of the Industry 118
§ 2. The Limits to Increases of Efficiency. . . 120
§ 3. The Mobility of Economies 124

CHAPTER X

THE LOCATION OF PRODUCTION
(1) NATIONAL

§ 1. Costs of Transport and Location . . . 127
§ 2. The Influence of Cheap Supplies of Factors of
Production 131

§ 3. Large Scale Production and Location . . 133
§ 4. Degrees of Industrial Concentration . . . 135
§ 5. The Influence of the Market 137

CHAPTER XI

THE LOCATION OF PRODUCTION
(2) INTERNATIONAL

§ 1. The Assumption of Immobility. . . . 138
§ 2. The International Division of Labour . . 138
§ 3. The Problem of Interference 140
§ 4. Infant Industries 142
§ 5. The Employment Argument 142
§ 6. The Key Industry Argument 143
§ 7. The Cost of Protection 144

CHAPTER XII

INTERVENTION TO IMPROVE EFFICIENCY

§ 1. The Scope of Intervention 146
§ 2. The Coercion of the Consumer. . . . 148
§ 3. Intervention to Mitigate the Severity of Competi-
    tion 152
§ 4. Competition or Control?. 154
§ 5. The Importance of Scale 155

CHAPTER I

INTRODUCTORY

§ 1. The Meaning of Industrial Efficiency. Great Britain is even to-day one of the richest countries in the world. The average income is as high or higher than that of most of the other countries of Europe. It is a dozen times higher than that of India. During the life-time of many of us it has risen very considerably. But even now there are many who live drab lives in conditions of great poverty. Their number is indeed smaller than a generation ago. None the less we need to increase industrial efficiency in order that we may raise our standards of consumption and have more resources available to do what may be wanted to modernise our industries, to improve our defences and to provide better social services. The effect of two wars has been to make us more dependent than we used to be on our own current efforts and more dependent on our power to produce and sell exports competitively with other nations. There are few problems confronting the nation which would not be very much easier to solve if production and national income were, let us say, 50 per cent higher than they are to-day. Such an increase is not impossible during a couple of decades if we make the best use both of our resources and of all the available scientific and engineering knowledge of this and other countries. Output per head in the industries of the United States is in most cases twice that of the same industries in this country, and in some cases as much as four times as great.

If we are concerned with this great problem of how we may best increase our national income so that all may have enough, we must start from a study of industrial efficiency, the securing of the greatest results at the least cost, and find to what forms of industrial structure efficiency will lead us.   But we must pause a moment to consider what exactly we mean by industrial efficiency. All industrial efficiency consists in trying to do with eight men what we have hitherto been doing with ten men.   It consists in creating unemployment.   But the ultimate purpose of increasing our national income is not complete until we have not only caused unemployment, but have also cured it.   We must use the men whom we have displaced to provide us with those things which we were before too poor to have.

The first stage, then, is the creating of unemployment. Great Britain is richer than other countries because we have learned to satisfy our most urgent needs with a smaller expenditure of effort and time. We have therefore the opportunity of producing and consuming things which other less fortunate countries cannot afford.   In some parts of India, a man can still be seen producing iron, sitting on his haunches with a blow-pipe and a little charcoal and a lump of ore.   It has been calculated that it would take a hundred thousand men by that method to produce what one modern blast furnace, worked by some thirty men, can turn out in the same time.   When Ford reorganised his works in 1921 he succeeded in reducing the number of workers employed for every car built daily from sixteen to nine.   Between 1920 and 1938 Cadbury's more than doubled the output per employee. Efficiency led to the release of workers, to the setting free of time and effort for new production, sometimes more of the same things, sometimes quite different things.

We often hear the argument that technical progress— 'automation' as some forms of it have now been christened— will throw workers out of employment. That is to argue in effect that there are no growing industries waiting to absorb the unemployed. But it has always been so. Nearly four million workers were employed in 1957 in industries which did not exist or hardly existed in 1900. If we had been looking for jobs for those workers in 1900, we should never have foreseen the present numbers of workers in the motor industry and motor transport, in the making of gramophones, wireless or television sets, in electricity, or aviation. At any moment it is hard to foresee how those workers will ultimately be absorbed, for whose services in their former occupations there is likely to be less demand. That is no reason for doubting their ultimate absorption, unless we doubt our own capacity to spend larger incomes than we at present enjoy. But it is one of the possible penalties of wealth that as a country gets richer and tends to save more of its income, it may become harder to absorb those who are unemployed through progress. The history of the decade since the Second World War both in America and in Europe does not suggest, however, that it is at present a major problem.

If we in Great Britain lived in a closed economic system which was completely within our own control, we might prefer from time to time to call a halt to invention; we might prefer to say 'until we have re-employed those whom we have at present unemployed, we will cause no more unemployment.' But, unfortunately, we do not live in a closed system. We live in an open and generally a very competitive world. If our competitors discover new and more economical ways of doing things, we must follow or lose our trade. Reorganisation is not optional for an industry whose foreign competitors have reorganised; it is the one alternative to extinction.

§ 2. Some Difficulties of Definition. In this book we shall be concerned with more modest problems than the broad strategies of economic policy. Any decision on such matters must involve a previous decision concerning the reactions of closed and open systems, of tariffs, or whatever it may be, upon the scale and efficiency of industries. The purpose of this book is to examine the forces which determine the size and structure of firms, and those further forces which determine the minimum efficient scale of an industry. It is hoped that an analysis of these problems will help to throw some light upon those more controversial questions of economic policies with which we are all concerned.

But before we start we must deal first with a problem which appears at first glance trivial, and capable of easy answer. What is an industry? If we are to discuss individual firms and their relations to their industry we must at least know what an industry is. But to define it with the accuracy on which we should insist is difficult. When we speak of the cotton industry, the iron and steel industry, even the motor industry, we are referring not to a group of firms producing what we may regard as a single commodity, but to many firms producing all sorts of different commodities, each firm very often producing several commodities inside a single plant. If we take the organisation which we commonly call the motor industry, is it a single industry producing a single commodity? Or is it several industries producing several commodities? We have some twenty firms, large and small, some of them branches of bigger groups, producing some fifty different models of passenger cars, apart from variations of bodywork. These fifty models fall into four broad groups of roughly similar price and horse-power. Are there fifty commodities, or four or one, produced by the motor industry? Is the British Motor Corporation making twelve different commodities, all of which compete with each other in the same market, or is it, inside its wide organisation, making twelve commodities, each with its own separate market, but with many common economies of manufacture?

Common sense, and a trust in the worldly wisdom of the B.M.C., lead us to prefer the latter conclusion, and it is the word 'market' which has brought us nearer to the solution of our problem. We should like to mean by an industry a group of firms producing the same commodity for the same market We know what we mean by a market. It has been defined for us as 'a region in which buyers and sellers are in such free intercourse with one another that the prices of the same goods tend to equality easily and quickly.' But in real life it is seldom that different producers produce 'the same goods.' Each one tries to create a separate market and a separate demand for his own goods by making them, if only in name, slightly different, and by cajoling the public by advertisement into thinking them different. Producers of pig-iron, of flour, of salt, of raisins, of boots, hats and arm-chairs, of petrol, oil and motor tyres, of everything we ever use, eat or wear, are continually engaged in breaking up the market into smaller markets, for which by natural advantage, by reputation, or patent, they have the sole supply. That is, they wish to create a separate demand for their own products. In a perfect market one individual producer must accept the market price, to the fixing of which he individually contributes, but contributes to an insignificant extent. If he attempts to make his price higher than the market price he will sell nothing. If he sets it at the market price he can sell more than all that he can produce. By creating a separate demand for his product, on the other hand, he is enabled to charge a price higher than the market price without losing the whole of the demand for it. Within certain narrow limits he can act as a monopolist of his goods.

There are to-day very few commodities for which a perfect or even approximately perfect market exists. By far the greater number of the things which we consume are branded, marked, identified into separate smaller markets. Competition is hardly anywhere now perfect, but though competition in the strictest sense is thus limited, it would be foolish to treat it as unimportant. Let us take two very similar motor-cars. They will have their separate markets; each will have its admirers, but each is a substitute for the other. At some difference of price, almost every potential purchaser can be attracted from the one to the other. And so the price fixing powers of the manufacturers of one are limited by the price fixing policy of the manufacturers of the other. Each is to a large degree a substitute for the other.

Substitutes may be either direct, as in this case, or indirect, as in many others. We balance the merits of a possible car not only against other cars, but against countless other ways of spending our money. The price fixing powers of the motor manufacturer are limited not only by other motor manufacturers, but by the cost of railway fares, of arm-chairs, television sets, foreign travel, or fur coats. The butchers of a certain large town complained some years ago that owing to the reduction in the price of motor-cars the demand for sirloins of beef had fallen off. Their customers bought a little meat paste for sandwiches for the Sunday picnic, and no longer the necessary preliminaries to a somnolent Sunday afternoon. The competition of almost identical goods is different in degree, rather than in kind, from the competition of more distant substitutes.

The interest of the small manufacturer, as we have seen, lies in breaking up the market into a number of small separate markets. The interest of the consumer lies in the opposite direction. He demands a combination of quality and cheapness. In the pursuit of quality, he is all too often deprived of cheapness. By the breaking up of the market into many small markets, the growth of the output of the most efficient firm to that scale which would afford the greatest possible efficiency is made difficult or impossible. We shall have to consider in a later chapter how far this breaking up of markets can be prevented by voluntary or official action. For the moment, we are concerned with the limit set on large-scale production by the extent of the market. There will be in any given area only a certain number of purchasers of any one commodity. The limit to the extent of the area which affords the market of any one producer may be either natural or artificial. The limit may be due to the impossibility of transporting goods without deterioration. The scale of production of ice tends even to-day to remain small because its value in proportion to its weight is small, and unless carried in special vehicles it is apt to cease to be ice. Bread is made locally, because new bread manufactured, let us say, for the whole country in Liverpool would have ceased to be new bread before it reached Land's End or John o' Groat's. Milk and market garden produce, in the same way, can bear only limited transport without similar deterioration.

The market may be limited also by artificial barriers. They may be barriers of preferences and prejudices, such as have already been described. They may be barriers of tariffs and prohibitions set up between one political area and another. Muddletown could, at one time, insist on the monopoly of its municipal electric light works, its gas works, or waterworks, however ill adapted to the requirements of its citizens, and turn a deaf ear to the proposals of neighbouring towns; even to-day it can still, if just large enough, insist on controlling its own educational system. Ruritania may prefer to create a narrow limited market within its own boundaries, and refuse to accept the efficient products of its neighbours. In both cases, maximum efficiency may be limited by a market politically determined.

Where these narrower limits to a market are not found, the limit lies in the cost of transport. The market of a single more efficient producing centre will extend up to the point where the gain in lower cost of production is balanced by a loss in greater cost of transport. The local less efficient producer will find a market in his own immediate neighbourhood, but his sphere of influence will be narrower than that of his larger rival. A small coal mine in an industrial area frequently enjoys a profitable local market, but is unable to compete with more efficient low cost undertakings in the national market.

A hundred and fifty years ago, Adam Smith described how 'upon two hundred tons of goods carried by the cheapest land-carriage from London to Edinburgh, there must be charged the maintenance of a hundred men for three weeks, and both the maintenance, and, what is nearly equal to the maintenance, the wear and tear of four hundred horses as well as of fifty great waggons.' In those days, had water transport not been available, little trade could have taken place between London and Edinburgh. To-day, for a thousand things, London and Edinburgh form a single land-joined market. As transport became cheaper during the nineteenth century, markets which had previously been separate became joined in a single market, and the appropriate location of the producing unit and the appropriate scale of the producing unit both changed. Cheap motor transport is still enlarging the possible markets of manufacturers and making large-scale production rather easier to attain.

It had seemed at first glance that it would be possible for us to define an industry as a group of firms producing the same commodity for the same market. We must now recognise that to define it either by the commodity produced, or by the market for which it produces, is in many cases either impossible or at least unsatisfactory. In practice, all that we can do is to follow the example of those who are actually engaged in industries. Certain employers find that they have a common bond of interest with certain other employers, and come to regard themselves as composing an industry. The bond may be one of the broad type of general product, as in the motor industry, the electrical industry, the paperbox industry. It may be one of a common use of a single raw material, as in the iron and steel industry, the pottery industry, the cotton industry. It may be one of a common use of a given type of machinery, or of a given process of manufacture. Thus we may distinguish the textile industries; we may speak of brass founders, or of steel rolling firms as having something in common which distinguishes them from other firms. Industries as such have no identity. They are simply a classification of firms which may for the moment be convenient. A change of technique and of organisation may require a new classification and a new industry. In the past few decades we have added the aircraft and radio industries, the rayon, plastics and electronics industries to our list.

These problems of industries, of markets and breaking up of markets, of substitutes both close and more distant, all have their importance when one comes to study monopoly, the strength and weakness of particular monopolies, and the stages between perfect competition and monopoly which have come, since this book was first published, to be known as imperfect competition and monopolistic competition. They have their chief place in the volume in this series called *Monopoly*. But we cannot fully understand those problems, or usefully study the damage that may be caused by monopoly unless we begin by studying the structure of firms and industries in a competitive market. That is the main theme of this book.

May I say a word finally about the 'firm'? In the greater part of this book I shall be discussing the factors which determine the size of 'firms'. I have deliberately chosen a word of wide coverage. In my view we have to be interested not only in the technical unit—the plant—but also in the units of management, of selling and buying, of capital raising, of risk-spreading, and so on. In some industries the ordinary unit of enterprise is a single plant, and any attempt to distinguish between the plant, as the technical unit, and the firm, as the financial, capital-raising and risk-spreading unit, is unnecessary. But in a good many other industries there is a tendency for the unit of enterprise to include several physically separate plants; if we are to understand industrial structure we must attempt to explain to ourselves why there should sometimes be advantage in this multiplication of technical units under a single ownership, and even on occasion also under a single management.

The main reasons why several plants may be combined in a single unit of enterprise will, I hope, emerge in the course of the next six chapters, and particularly in Chapter VII. For the moment it is sufficient to make clear that the word 'firm' will be here used in this wider sense of the unit of finance and enterprise.

CHAPTER II

THE OPTIMUM FIRM

§ **1. The Concept of the Optimum Firm.** In this and the succeeding chapters, I shall be concerned with the best size of the producing unit, the optimum scale both of the firm and of the industry. I shall deal first with the optimum firm. In any industry there is usually to be found sometimes one, sometimes more than one size to which a firm has apparently tended to grow. This size, which Alfred Marshall taught us to call the 'representative' firm, may not be the optimum at the moment; circumstances may have so changed that some size, perhaps slightly different, perhaps, as is not improbably the case in the cotton industry to-day, wholly different from the older one, is now to be preferred. The representative firm of to-day probably represents the scale of production which, having regard to the circumstances of the industry, was looked upon as the best scale of production sometime in the recent past.

We in this country have rather more information now than we did a generation ago, thanks mainly to the improvements of the Census of Production. But even now we have much less information than is available for the United States. One of the best analyses of size, which has the added advantage of measuring size by a physical unit of capacity rather than by employment as does the Census of Production, is for the cotton industry, and is derived from an enquiry, now many years old, made by Sir Sydney Chapman and Professor Ashton.[1] One example from that enquiry may be given. In 1911, there were 408 joint stock spinning firms, ranging in size

[1] See Report of (Balfour) Committee on Industry and Trade—Survey of Textile Industries, p. 144.

from 2,500 spindles to over 260,000 spindles. Of these 408 firms, 51 firms lay within the range of 90,000 to 100,000 spindles, 120 firms between 80,000 and 110,000, and 185 firms between 70,000 and 120,000 spindles. We may then regard the size of 100,000 spindles as being the typical unit of that date, representing what the cotton industry had regarded as the optimum scale at the time when those mills had been erected. We should be wrong in regarding it as necessarily the optimum in 1911. Firms of over 200,000 spindles had increased from none in 1884 to 14 in 1911, and the optimum at the latter date was not improbably to be found in this class. To-day, as we shall see in a later chapter, the optimum unit in the cotton industry may not impossibly be widely different from this, and require a control of several millions of spindles.

By the optimum firm, we must mean a firm operating at that scale at which in existing conditions of technique and organising ability it has the lowest average cost of production per unit, when all those costs which must be covered in the long run are included. I am not for the moment concerned with questions of maximum profitability. When an element of monopoly is present, the price need not coincide with average cost, and maximum profit may be made by charging a price at which the firm does not sell enough to exhaust the full economies of scale. I am here concerned only with costs and the relation of costs to size. The establishment of this optimum firm will be in part the result of conscious decision by business men who are considering how they most profitably can invest their resources; in part it will be the product of the forces of competition, which tend, as a rule, to eliminate the inefficient and to encourage the efficient. Both these elements play their part because competition only indirectly gives an advantage to the firm with the lowest average long period cost of production. Short period competition tends as a rule to select the firm whose short period cost of production is lowest. And since capital equipment is long-lived, and available in the short period whether or not it is sufficiently rewarded, economies of capital costs play little part in short period competition. But in a longer period, capital wears out and must be replaced, and investors will consciously seek out that size of plant and firm which, over a period of years, offers the best return on their capital. The longer period competition of investors will tend, therefore, to perpetuate that firm which enjoys the lowest average cost of production. It is with this long period optimum firm that I am here concerned.

The optimum firm is likely to result from the ordinary play of economic forces where the market is perfect and sufficient to maintain a large number of firms of optimum size. It will not necessarily emerge where the market is limited and imperfect. If a firm, to secure additional sales, must attract customers, either from rival products or from greater distances, by accepting a lower price, that firm may actually decrease and not increase its profits by expanding to the optimum size. In these circumstances, it will be likely to remain at that smaller size at which its additional receipts from selling more are equal to its additional costs in producing more.

The forces which determine the best size of the business unit, assuming that the market is sufficient to absorb the whole production of at least one firm of optimum size, may be divided into five main categories: technical forces, making for a technical optimum size; managerial forces, making for an optimum managerial unit; financial forces, making for an optimum financial unit; the influences of marketing, making for an optimum sales unit; and the forces of risk and fluctuation, making for a unit possessing the greatest power of survival in the face of industrial vicissitudes. These five forces may, in certain cases, lead to an approximately similar optimum size. In other cases, the benefits of growth on the technical side may balance losses from growth through the building up of an industrial unit too large to be managed with the highest degree of efficiency and flexibility. The advantage of a large unit for selling may in yet other cases be balanced by the disadvantage of large productive units in time of depression.   In a later chapter, I shall attempt to show how conflicts between the best technical scale and the best managerial scale can be resolved by different devices and forms of organisation.

§ 2. The Division of Labour and the Size of the Optimum Technical Unit. It is convenient to start by considering the various factors which determine the technical optimum scale of production. The first principle of which we must take account is that of the Division of Labour. In his famous first chapter of *The Wealth of Nations*, Adam Smith has described the various advantages to be secured by the Division of Labour. Adam Smith takes his example 'from a very trifling manufacture; but one in which the division of labour has been very often taken notice of, the trade of the pin-maker; a workman not educated to this business (which the division of labour has rendered a distinct trade), nor acquainted with the use of the machinery employed in it (to the invention of which the same division of labour has probably given occasion), could scarce, perhaps, with his utmost industry, make one pin in a day, and certainly could not make twenty. But in the way in which this business is now carried on, not only the whole work is a peculiar trade, but it is divided into a number of branches, of which the greater part are likewise peculiar trades. One man draws out the wire, another straights it, a third cuts it, a fourth points it, a fifth grinds it at the top for receiving the head; to make the head requires two or three distinct operations; to put it on is a peculiar business, to whiten the pins is another; it is even a trade by itself to put them into the paper; and the important business of making a pin is, in this manner, divided into about eighteen distinct operations, which, in some manufactories, are all performed by distinct hands, though in others the same man will sometimes perform two or three of them.

'I have seen a small manufactory of this kind where ten men only were employed, and where some of them consequently performed two or three distinct operations. But though they were very poor, and therefore but indifferently accommodated with the necessary machinery, they could, when they exerted themselves, make among them about twelve pounds of pins in a day. There are in a pound upwards of four thousand pins of a middling size. Those ten persons, therefore, could make among them upwards of forty-eight thousand pins in a day. Each person, therefore, making a tenth part of forty-eight thousand pins, might be considered as making four thousand eight hundred pins in a day. But if they had all wrought separately and independently, and without any of them having been educated to this peculiar business, they certainly could not each of them have made twenty, perhaps not one pin in a day; that is, certainly, not the two hundred and fortieth, perhaps not the four thousand eight hundredth part of what they are at present capable of performing, in consequence of a proper division and combination of their different operations."[1]

Since Adam Smith's day, mechanical and industrial progress has led us to more and more minute division of labour. A pair of shoes is made now by groups of men and women working at some 240 different operations. The manufacture of watches, typewriters, motor cars, is broken up into many tiny parts. Even the old model T Ford was, according to its designer, the product of 7,882 different jobs. More simple products are incapable of such fine subdivision. A table knife, or a loaf of bread could not with advantage pass through a thousand hands, however large the output to be produced; a dozen or so could do the work as well. But a motor car could not be cheaply manufactured by a dozen men, however skilled, though some of the finest racing cars are made that way.

We shall see later the effects of this maximum profitable subdivision upon the size of the firms; we must study first the effects of division of labour. Why is it that the division of labour makes for more efficient production? Adam Smith may again be called to our assistance. He distinguishes three

[1] Adam Smith, *Wealth of Nations*, Book I, Chapter I. (Cannan's edition, pp. 6–7.)

different reasons for the increase in the quantity of work which, in consequence of the division of labour, a given number of people are capable of performing. It is owing 'first, to the increase of dexterity in every particular workman; secondly, to the saving of the time which is commonly lost in passing from one species of work to another; and lastly, to the invention of a great number of machines which facilitate and abridge labour, and enable one man to do the work of many.'

Let us consider first the question of dexterity. A man or woman who works continuously at one task for some time will acquire a skill or a knack of doing it which will not be shared by another, even naturally more skilful, who has not tackled that job before. A rhythm of work and an economy of motion may be evolved, or learned from an expert, which will make the work less fatiguing, and enable the worker to keep up a high rate of output for a longer period. Less thought and concentration will be necessary to ensure that each movement is that which is next required, until the whole action becomes automatic. To this acquired dexterity which Adam Smith has described must be added also the opportunity which is offered by the division of labour of specialising persons with particular natural gifts or qualities upon the work which they are best fitted to perform, and of specialising those who have defects of skill or physique upon those tasks in which their impediments are least damaging to their efficiency. There were 7,882 jobs in the Ford factory. 'Of these, 949 were classified as heavy work requiring strong, able-bodied and practically physically perfect men; 3,338 required men of ordinary physical development and strength. The remaining 3,595 jobs were disclosed as requiring no physical exertion, and could be performed by the slightest, weakest sort of men. In fact, most of them could be satisfactorily filled by women or older children. The lightest jobs were again classified to discover how many of them require the use of full faculties, and we found that 670 could be filled by legless men, 2,637 by one-legged men, 2 by armless men, 715 by one-armed men, and 10 by blind men.'[1] It is a waste to employ a skilled craftsman on work that a child might equally well do; it is a waste to employ a skilled accountant on work which a typist ought to be doing. In a large firm, a skilled man can be kept all the time employed on work which requires all his abilities. In a small firm, he may spend much of his day on tasks which a less skilled and cheaper worker could equally well perform.

Adam Smith discovered a second economy in the saving of time which is lost in passing from one task to another. A weaver, who in those days combined that work with the cultivation of a small farm, would waste, he said, much of his time in travelling from one task to the other. In a more mechanised world, the same losses are to be discovered where men move from machine to machine or from one process to another process in manufacture. A similar loss is to be found in the case of machines which must be re-set to perform some different function, to roll a different section in a steel rolling mill, to machine a different part of a motor car or a weighing machine, to spin a different count of cotton yarn, or to weave a different cloth. The steady flow of production is interrupted if rolls must be changed or looms re-set. It is by securing the steady concentration of man and machine upon a single task that the division of labour achieves economy, and the large firm enjoys an advantage over the small firm just in so far as it makes this concentration possible. The advantage is the greater, the greater the loss in turning over from operation to operation. In those many industrial operations in which the machine must be nicely adjusted before it will turn out satisfactory work, the cost of change-over may be considerable. A large steel press may take many hours of adjustment before it is perfectly set, and spoil valuable material in the meanwhile. In other industries, and with other machines, the change-over may be so quick that comparatively little time is lost, and the gain to be secured by specialisation of machinery is proportionately reduced. It has even been

[1] Ford, *My Life and Work,* p. 108.

claimed that in some cases the change of task is beneficial in reducing monotony, and stimulating the interest of the workers.

The third economy which Adam Smith has distinguished is that due to the development of specialised machinery to perform the different tasks into which the manufacture has been divided. By the separation of a single process, and its analysis into its constituent parts, the task of devising a machine to take over much or all of the labour and skill of the worker is facilitated. The boy who pulled a string controlling the valve of one of the first engines discovered how, if he tied it to a certain part of the engine, his absence might pass unnoticed, and by doing so invented valve gears. Many of the small inventions which have done much to simplify machinery, or to make it more nearly automatic, have been the work of operators who, during the hours of tending a machine, have consciously or unconsciously analysed their own part in the rhythm of the operation, and have found a way of throwing yet another task on to the machine itself.

The principle of the division of labour requires, then, a firm sufficiently large to obtain the maximum profitable division of labour. The size necessary to obtain this will be different even in different industries; it will be different even in different departments of the same manufacture. In some instances, a further division of labour is by the very nature of the process impossible. In cotton spinning, the sequence of processes has long been divided into the greatest number technically possible. In weaving, a further subdivision of the operations of the loom is unthinkable. The large spinning or weaving firm differs hardly at all in equipment from its small competitor, but a firm of less than 20,000 spindles would probably be unable to keep running at full capacity certain of the larger units of its machinery. In other instances, the maximum subdivision of processes is achieved in some departments while the scale of production is comparatively small, while other departments continue to secure further subdivision of labour as the scale of production increases.

If two engineering firms, for instance, be compared, the one large, the other on modern standards rather small, the division of labour in the machine shops may be found to extend little further in the large firm than in the small. It happens only seldom, though in the motor industry more often than in most industries, that a single worker or a single machine handles the whole output of one component. In most instances, several workers will be simultaneously doing the same work on a series of similar machines. In the large shop there will be more, in the small fewer such machines; the division of labour will not be greater in the one than in the other, and, were it possible, division of labour could be secured as readily in the smaller as in the larger firm. But at other points such division of labour is possible.

If one compares two motor firms, one large, one small, the large firm possesses an elaborate assembly line; here one worker or group of workers perform for the whole output of the firm that particular job for which they are responsible. The smaller firm has a more rudimentary assembly line. Each worker performs several tasks, which in a larger firm are divided between several men. In this case, then, there is a gain from a larger scale of production, but the gain is limited to those processes where further subdivision is possible only if the firm grows bigger. If the subdivision could be achieved by replacing two men both simultaneously doing the whole job by two men each doing a different portion of the job, it is unnecessary for the firm to grow to secure the division. It is only necessary to increase the scale of production in order to obtain further division of labour if the whole output is already handled by a single man or a single machine, and the necessary division of labour cannot be obtained by a mere re-arrangement of their tasks. In the particular and very exceptional case of the motor industry very large scale continues to give economies. For certain processes an output of something like 400,000 units a year must be reached before duplication is necessary.

This type of situation is, on the whole, rare; in most industries to-day, the full possibilities of the division of labour can be realised in a unit far smaller than the units which are commonly found. To take one illustration, safety-razor blades are made by a standard set of machines, each of which handles only a small fraction of the output of a plant. A large plant has many machines, a small plant has fewer. But the technique and the division of labour differs hardly at all between the large plant and the small plant. For the moment, that is to say, the technical economies of the division of labour have been exhausted even in a relatively small plant.

§ 3. **The Integration of Processes.** We must then search for other technical gains from large scale production. The first that we discover has not yet, so far as I know, been christened. I am going to call it the Integration of Processes. The large firm often differs from the small firm in having fewer rather than more processes of manufacture. The process of the division of labour is being reversed; one large machine can be designed to take over what has hitherto been done by a series of manual, or less completely mechanical operations. Twenty years ago in a small motor factory, panels were usually beaten out laboriously by hand. Now in any large factory an enormous press is kept busily occupied, supplanting the room full of panel beaters, and that and a few welders take the place of the many processes of earlier methods of body making. In other cases, two or three or more consecutive processes are performed by a more complicated automatic transfer machine, which thereby eliminates the labour and time required to set up the work on each of the successive earlier machines.

It is only the large firm that can afford to keep the very expensive machinery of this type running to its full capacity, and the large firm therefore enjoys advantages which are beyond the reach of the self-contained small firm.

§ 4. **Vertical Disintegration.** The small firm has a means of escape from the difficulty described in the last paragraph, an escape very confusing to our attempt to analyse the structure of an industry. Where some given process requires a scale of production considerably greater than the smaller firms in an industry can achieve, this process tends to be separated off from the main industry, and all the smaller firms to get this particular process performed for them by an outside specialist firm. Thus the industry becomes broken up into two or more industries, and each is enabled to work at its most convenient scale of production. The specialist firm, working for a number of the smaller firms, is on a larger scale than any of the individual firms could have achieved for that particular process or product. Examples of this principle may be found in the finishing stages of the textile industries, and in the manufacture of various component parts, such as radiators, electrical equipment, body shells, and crankshafts and other forgings, in the motor industry.

This method of escaping the limitations of particular processes by breaking the continuity of production from first to last within a single firm, I am going to call Vertical Disintegration, to distinguish it from the similar but opposite expedient of Vertical Integration, which consists in the combination of one stage of production with other previously separated stages of production, under the control of a single firm. Its importance lies in its power to eliminate the advantages of very large scale production, where those advantages are limited to one or two processes of manufacture. But it is not a practicable method of escape where the advantages are too many, or where the processes cannot by their nature be separated and given to an outside firm, as in the case of motor car assembly work. In these instances, the advantages of the Integration of Processes must, other things being equal, form a factor favourable to further growth of the firm.

§ 5. The Economy of the Large Machine. The gain from the Integration of Processes arose from the unification of a number of processes hitherto performed in series, so that they might be performed simultaneously. A somewhat similar economy will arise also where, when output has sufficiently increased, one process which has hitherto been performed by a number of parallel workers may be taken over by a single machine. Once a machine has been developed to perform some duty, an economy lies with those who can afford to employ it. Some machines are cheap, and can be supplied as tools to every worker, since the saving of time when he needs them will pay for their cost. Others are expensive, and no firm can afford them unless it can operate them continuously. The interest and depreciation on a large steel press may amount to more than £100 per day, and it will clearly not pay to have it standing idle; but no one would suggest that it is wasteful for me to have a separate telephone because I do not speak down it continuously, and that a single telephone for the whole of my street would be more economical. With a cheap and simple tool, the saving lies in having it close at hand, so that it saves the workers' time. With the expensive tool, economical operation depends on the spreading of its cost over as many units of output as possible during its working life. Obviously a large firm will be in a better position than a small firm to keep expensive machinery occupied, and will gain either in that it can afford to buy machinery which, for the smaller scale of operation, is so costly as to be unprofitable, or while using similar machinery, it will be able to assign a smaller share of the expenses of the machinery to each unit of product that is turned out.

We must consider for a moment what are the factors that determine the gain from using machines more fully. The greater is the fixed cost per day of possessing a given machine, the greater will be the economy from spreading that cost over a larger output. The fixed cost per day will depend first upon the price of the machine, second on the rate of interest and depreciation which must be paid. If something happens to reduce the cost of the machine, or to lower the rate of interest, the penalty for working it below its full capacity is reduced, and the advantage to the large firm which can so employ it is less. Moreover, for some machines the depreciation is mainly the result of wear and tear, for others it is the result of obsolescence. Where wear and tear is the only factor, the smaller firm, using its machine over a longer period, must pay higher interest charges, but not a higher proportion of the initial cost of the machine, for each unit of product. Where obsolescence is important, the small firm working its equipment below the full capacity of the machinery must pay both a higher interest charge and a higher proportion of the initial cost.

We can see then that the optimum firm is not an absolute and unchanging thing. Its size will vary not only with changes of technique but also with changes in the price of machines, the rate of interest, and the rate of invention in a given industry. If any of these changes, the optimum firm changes also. Equally if the cost of operative labour changes relatively to the cost of machinery the optimum size of the firm is affected.

The economies to be secured from the integration of processes, and from the spreading of the overhead costs of large machines, give us a hint to another factor which helps to determine the technical optimum. We have so far been considering plant whose minimum size is capable of dealing with a large output. But in other cases, we can see that while a smaller mechanical unit is technically possible, a larger one may be more efficient. Both a large and a small electrical power-station are technically possible, but the large station has an advantage in efficiency over the small station. We may then ask whether in general it is true that large mechanical units have an advantage over smaller ones, and, if they do, why it should be so. In certain cases they have an advantage, and the reasons are two, the first technical, the second concerned with the necessary labour supply.

The technical advantage is quite simple once it is understood. If you take an ordinary container, such as a water tank, and double every dimension, so that it is twice as high, twice as long and twice as broad as it was before, the amount of water which the tank will hold has increased with the cube of the dimension; that is, in this case it has increased eight times. But the area of the walls of the tank will only have increased as the square of the dimension. In this case it will have increased four times. Now, if you are building a furnace, or any container in which things have to be kept either hot or cold, this is important, for radiation is dependent upon the area of the walls. It explains why, up to a certain limit, the advantage lies with the large blast furnace, the large steel furnace, the large glass furnace; but in each case, certain other technical considerations come in which limit the possible growth in this direction. A blast furnace cannot with advantage be larger than a certain size, which may vary from district to district, because the strength of the locally available coke is insufficient to carry a burden of greater amount without becoming crushed, and impeding the necessary passage of air through the furnace; the cost of better coke would exceed the saving of larger size.

Where the object has to be moved against the resistance of water or air, as in the case of a ship or of an aircraft, similar gains are to be found, for while the capacity of a ship increases with the cube of its dimensions, the resistance increases in proportion approximately to the wetted area, which increases as the square of the dimensions. A large ship will, therefore, require less horse-power per ton to move it at a given speed, or with the same horse-power per ton will travel faster than a smaller ship. If the lower speed is sufficient, there is a saving in the proportion of the ship devoted to engine space. And similarly with an aircraft. If all the dimensions are doubled, the cubic content and thus the passenger space in a civil aircraft will increase eight-fold. The resistance will increase about four-fold. Thus the larger aircraft, if of similar form and with similar horsepower per ton, will be faster than the smaller aircraft. But this gain cannot be exploited indefinitely, for the wing area which provides the lift will have increased only four-fold and the minimum landing speed of the larger aircraft will thus be higher and the runway necessary for take-off and landing will be longer.[1]

So far, we have discussed only the technical efficiency of the large unit as compared with that of the small. We are concerned also with the cost of the large unit as compared with the cost of the small. If the large unit, though technically more efficient, were more expensive to construct per unit of its future output of service, this gain might disappear; but in practice the larger unit is nearly always relatively cheaper to construct than the smaller. If we compare the capital cost of two electrical generating stations, one of the largest efficient size, the other of small size, each representing about the same technical development, we find that the smaller station costs almost twice as much, for each kilowatt of capacity, as the larger station.

To take another more homely example, a cistern to hold 25 gallons costs £3, one to hold 250 gallons £12. The explanation is, of course, that the large unit takes more material, but not proportionately more labour to construct. The labour required to build the 1,500 c.c. B.M.C. engine is not half as much again as that required to build the very similar 900 c.c. B.M.C. engine. In many cases, also, the thickness of the wall of the container, neither for reasons of strength nor for insulation, need be increased in the same proportion as the other dimensions. An economy of structural material is therefore possible.

It is clear that, in many cases, the large mechanical unit is both more efficient in operation and cheaper to construct than the smaller. It has, as was indicated above, a second advantage; it is cheaper also, in many cases, to operate, for many machines require an individual or a team to work them, whatever their size may be. A steel furnace, a rolling mill, a locomotive, a power house, requires a team which within a wide range of output varies comparatively little. The same

[1] The reader is referred to J. M. Clark, *The Economics of Overhead Costs*, p. 116, for the cautionary tale of the man who hoped to increase the size of the plough.

locomotive crew works the five-hundred-ton train of the Royal Scot and the fifty-ton train of the Talyllyn Railway.   To turn a valve, to operate a switch, or to watch a gauge is a no more arduous, though much more responsible, labour for a huge power station than for a tiny plant.   An important economy of the larger civil aircraft as compared with the smaller is that, in relation to the number of passengers carried, the cost of the necessary aircrew is substantially less.

§ 6. The Balance of Processes.   It will be seen, then, that in very many cases an increase in the size of the mechanical unit gives an increase of efficiency, and that if the greatest technical efficiency is to be achieved, the size of the firm must be sufficient to use the largest mechanical unit necessary to its full capacity.   But here again a complication arises.   Mechanical units do not arrange themselves easily into groups such that they give their best results with an output, one of one hundred units a day, another of two hundred, a third of four hundred, so that they can be fitted neatly into the industrial jig-saw.   There will be several different mechanical bottle-necks in the firm, each requiring to be used, for greatest efficiency, up to its fullest capacity, but each requiring a different daily output in order that it may be so used.   The escape from this difficulty may be a compromise, one machine being over-driven, so that it produces slightly more than it can with optimum efficiency, another producing slightly less.   Where the difference between the optimum outputs is small, this will very likely be the solution adopted, but where the optimum outputs are considerably different for the two mechanical units, the best solution may be a kind of L.C.M. of all the various outputs, in which three units of one machine, four of another, five of a third, give a balance in which all the units can conveniently be used approximately to their full capacity.

This problem of the balance between different processes and different departments often exercises an important influence on scale in the iron and steel industry, where a proper balance between blast furnaces, coke ovens, waste gas utilisation, steel furnaces and rolling mills has to be obtained. Where it is likely that certain units will have to be closed down at intervals for repair, the effects of this upon the economies of the whole organisation must be considered. A small steel plant depending upon a single blast furnace, even if technically efficient while the latter was operating, would be liable to disorganisation whenever repair became necessary. For this among other reasons, steel plants consist usually of a small number of similar units operated together. The problem of the balance of equipment may be seen again in the lay-out of a cotton-spinning firm. A mill of about 100,000 mule spindles will employ, perhaps, one bale breaker, two double openers, four single scutchers, one hundred carding engines, some twelve drawing frames, eight slubbing frames, nineteen intermediate frames, fifty-two jack frames, eighty mules. A cotton firm must be of such size that all these various units may be conveniently combined without any wastes from partially employed equipment.

§ 7. **Economies of Massed Reserves.** There is a final type of economy that industry enjoys in common with military strategy. Where there is risk of breakdown of plant it is necessary to hold reserves, either in the form of equipment or in the form of stocks of semi-finished goods, to tide the firm over the interruption. Equally where demand is erratic and unpredictable, reserves, either of capacity or stocks, have to be held to meet the peak demand. If, for some technical reason, it is difficult to hold stocks, enough reserve capacity must be available to meet the whole emergency. If firms or other productive organisations are small, each must separately possess enough reserve to meet the breakdown of the largest unit, or the biggest increase of demand that may fall upon it. If a number of firms or productive organisations are amalgamated, they will be very unlikely to need the same total of reserves as were held before by the individual units. The economy of massed reserves is familiar to the soldier. It is equally familiar to those concerned with electricity supply.

One of the great economies of the electricity grid and the unification of all electricity supply has been that there has been a
very great reduction in the amount of reserve and stand-by
plant that has been required. Different towns and different
areas have peaks of demand at different times of the year. A
break-down in one area can be met by help from another area.
Similarly the pooling of locomotives and rolling-stock by all
the railways means that large emergency needs can draw upon
stock that is available anywhere in the country. The same
principle can also be applied with a large industrial organisation. A firm like Unilevers and Imperial Chemical Industries
can use capacity in one plant to help out another overloaded
plant. And within a firm, the big firm needs less proportionate reserve of machinery or of stocks to meet possible
emergencies than does the small firm.

§ 8. Economies through the Large Organisation.   If a firm is
to achieve the economies that have been set out in this chapter,
how should it go about it?   There are in effect two routes by
which it may attempt to reach its objective. First, it may
attempt to secure a large scale of operation by producing within
one plant or group of plants a number of products.   Second,
it may attempt to achieve the greatest possible standardisation
of its products.   It is important to see the extent to which
each of these can provide a solution.

Some of the economies of large scale can be achieved by
any plant that is large, irrespective of the degree of standardisation.   A large cotton mill or a large engineering works
can keep large units of unspecialised machinery operating continuously and obtain many of the advantages of division of
labour and specialisation of workers on the types of work for
which they have comparative advantages.   Equally it can
secure many of the economies of massed reserves; of employing workers on tasks for which they have a special aptitude;
of organisation to keep work running smoothly and continuously; of common services of transport; of canteen and other
facilities and many other economies which derive from the

fact that the firm is big rather than from the fact that it is producing a narrow range of products.

§ 9. Economies through Standardisation. Many economies, however, derive from the fact that output is concentrated on a few products. This is the objective of standardisation. It is convenient to begin by distinguishing two different concepts, both of which are important. The first is the establishment of standards to make components made by different manufacturers interchangeable. Thus we have camera films of standard sizes made by all manufacturers which will fit all cameras taking that size. We have standard electric fitments so that electric-light bulbs fit holders and so on. We have standard threads for sparking plugs, standard sizes of bricks and window frames, and of countless other things. It is an immense saving of time to both manufacturers and consumers if one can be certain that any component will fit as required.

But this standardisation, though very important in reducing the range of stocks to be carried and thus in narrowing the necessary range of products, is far less important than the standardisation by individual manufacturers of the things that they produce and the reduction of the number of varieties produced. It is this which offers the greatest scope for economy. Adam Smith, in the passage quoted above, drew attention to 'the time that is commonly lost in passing from one species of work to another.' With modern techniques the loss is very much greater. If work is absolutely rigidly standardised, the operative can be assisted in the light engineering industries by a great array of jigs and tools, of automatic transfer machines designed to do one job and capable of being adapted to another only at great expense; great presses may have moulds which cost many thousands of pounds to make and set up. Even in industries which do not lend themselves to these methods, there are very great economies to be obtained.

If we are to understand these economies, we must make one important distinction. Large scale production may take either or both of two forms. It may imply a large rate of flow of production; it may imply a long period over which a given flow of production is continued. Some production is organised on a flow basis; it is assumed that the flow will continue uninterrupted over a period of a year or so and the rate of flow is designed to meet the expected sales over that period. In these days almost all motor car production is organised on this basis; a considerable amount of the production of the radio industry, of the chemical industry and of other industries where there are long runs of a standard product is similarly organised. In other industries output is normally on the basis of a batch. A department is instructed to produce so many units of some product; when it has completed the batch it proceeds to re-set its equipment, if necessary, and to prepare to produce a batch of some other product. If more copies are wanted of one book than of another, there is no fundamental difference in the methods of composition and make-ready but the machines in the last stage continue to print for a longer period.

Some of the economies of large scale derive from a larger rate of flow. Further division of labour and specialisation can be obtained, as we have seen, in some cases only if the amount produced per day is larger. Some of the economies derive from a longer continuity of production. If there is a given cost of composing and correcting the type for a book, the cost of each copy will be reduced the larger the number of copies over which the overhead cost can be spread. And equally the cost of a car will be less if customers are prepared to allow the manufacturer to spread the very high cost of tooling-up and preparing moulds, dies and special equipment of every sort over, let us say, five years' output rather than three years' output.

In thinking of standardisation, therefore, one needs to think both of the extent to which the number of varieties can be reduced at any moment and also of the intervals at which change is demanded. In the United States, manufacturers have gone much further in reducing the number of varieties

than have manufacturers in most industries in the United
Kingdom. On the other hand they almost always change
design more rapidly.

How far is it desirable to go in the direction of reducing
variety? If we are to answer that question, we must find
what is the cost of variety. It is clearly desirable on the one
hand that the customer should be able to get as nearly as
possible the thing that he wants. On the other hand we all
lose if freedom to get the thing we want means that it is
immensely more expensive than it need have been. If we
had all accepted standardisation and had got the goods at the
price made possible thereby, we might all have been happier.
In some cases the cost of variety is not very great. At intervals a machine must in any case be stopped and re-set. It
costs relatively little more to re-set it on a different design.
It is not clear that if all shoes or all textile fabrics or all
china were rigidly standardised, the saving of cost would be
great. On the other hand the economies of standardising
components of motor cars, locomotives, bicycles and the like
are immense. In these cases it is often possible to provide
variety simultaneously with many of the advantages of standardisation by rigid standardisation of components combined
with a good deal of variety of detail and of parts where small
scale production is not seriously inefficient. That method of
trying to get the best of both worlds has been adopted both
by General Motors in America and by the British Motor
Corporation.

§ **10. The Trend of Size.** It is often said that industry is always
moving towards larger and larger scale. This is of course
true in some degree of some of the spectacular industries such
as the motor industry and chemicals, where the vast assembly
plants on the one hand and the vast cathedrals of chemical
engineering on the other impress our imaginations. The
statistical evidence is, however, far less clear. It must, moreover, be remembered that even in the motor industry only
about three-fifths of the output that goes into the final car

comes from these vast plants; about two-fifths represents the work embodied in parts bought in from outside firms organised, on average, on a very much smaller scale.

In the United Kingdom the proportion of all employees working in factories in the manufacturing trades employing 1,000 workers or more was 21·5 per cent in 1935; it had risen to 30·7 per cent in 1951. In 1935 about half the workers were employed in factories employing over 300 workers; the same proportion was employed in 1951 in factories employing over 400 workers. But in almost all countries the actual numbers of factories are increasing rather than diminishing. Small firms continue to come into existence and to find activities in which they can engage. For the United Kingdom we have no statistics that can yield safe comparisons over a long period; since 1935 the number of manufacturing establishments has increased by something like 10 per cent. In the United States the average number of workers per establishment remained surprisingly steady over the whole period 1914–39. If allowance is made for the increase of the volume of production per head, it is clear that there has been some increase of size measured in terms of output, but the average increase is of the order of 50–100 per cent rather than the astronomical increases that one might guess from thinking only in terms of the giants. It has been said that even to-day 'considerably more than one-half of the manufacturing output of the western world is produced in factories employing less than 500 workers.'[1]

§ 11. The Relation of the Optimum Technical Unit to the Optimum Firm. We have seen in this chapter that the large unit possesses many advantages over the small unit. The size of the optimum technical unit will depend upon how far these economies continue. They will not continue indefinitely. A large furnace is more economical than a small

[1] See Professor J. Jewkes in *The Economic Consequences of the Size of Nations*, Macmillan, 1959, and also the same author "The Size of the Factory", *Economic Journal*, June 1952.

furnace, but a point comes beyond which further growth is uneconomical. A large ship is faster and more economical than a small ship, but a point is reached beyond which an increase of size is an impediment rather than an advantage. Docks and canals are limited in capacity. The depth of water available may be insufficient for the safe operation of very large vessels. In other instances, further economies of the division of labour or of the integration of processes cease to arise, for the greatest possible advantage of existing technique has been secured. Another invention might perhaps necessitate a larger unit, perhaps even a unit vastly different, but for the time being there is no technical advantage in further growth.

Optimum technical units are large in two wholly different types of industry: in those in which the product or the productive machinery is physically very large, as in steel making, the rolling of steel plates and sections, or ship building: and in those in which the final product is highly complex in that it is built up of a great number of small parts, which are conveniently produced under a single roof, as in the case of the manufacture of typewriters, watches, cash registers, or motor cars. Optimum technical units are small where the product is both small and simple, as in the case of the manufacture of cutlery, the weaving of standard cloths, or the baking of bread. Thus we can predict, to some extent and within a given stage of technical development, the probable upper limit of the optimum technical unit in an industry. But we cannot be dogmatic concerning the limit to the growth of efficiency with size. The integration of processes is essentially discontinuous. There comes a point where, as output grows, a revolution of method becomes possible, and economies, which had for a period apparently ceased, again begin to arise with further growth.

But even where economies of larger scale cease completely, it is unlikely that countervailing diseconomies will begin to arise on the purely technical side. Thus the technical costs of production are likely to fall as more is produced up to a

certain limit, and thereafter to remain constant. So the technical optimum, though it establishes a minimum scale of
efficient operation, contributes hardly, if at all, to the fixing of
a maximum scale beyond which growth will lead to progressively increasing cost per unit. If other considerations require
a scale larger than the technical optimum, the technical scale
of production can be increased by mere multiplication, until
it coincides with that scale which these other considerations
would demand.

CHAPTER III

THE OPTIMUM MANAGERIAL UNIT

§ **1. Managerial Division of Labour.** In the last chapter we considered the effects of technical considerations upon the optimum size of a firm. In this chapter we will proceed to consider the effects of methods of management on the optimum size. Let us consider first what are the gains to be obtained on the side of management by an increased scale of production. We saw in the case of the technical methods of production that as a firm grows certain economies become possible. We were able to group these economies into certain types, and prominent among them were two, which we called the Division of Labour and the Integration of Processes. These economies are not limited in their sphere to technical methods of production. We find them also appearing in the management of large firms.

Let us consider first the possibilities of the division of labour. In a small works the manager has many different functions to perform. He must see an opening where a new enterprise can be expected to succeed, he must possess or secure capital, he must choose the best site for his plant, he must decide what equipment to install, and arrange its most efficient lay-out. He must design the goods that he is to produce, and prepare the necessary drawings; he must buy materials, estimate costs, and fix his price. He must organise and supervise production, instruct his workers as to how the goods shall be made, inspect them when made for defects, arrange their packing and transport, and collect payment. He must keep the factory accounts and see where profits are being made and where losses, he must work out the depreciation of the plant, and negotiate with the rapacious Inland

34

Revenue authorities. He must persuade unwilling and sus-
picious bankers or investors to lend him money, producers of
raw materials to give him credit, middlemen to buy his goods.
He ought, no doubt, to have time and patience to read those
invaluable articles in which journalists, politicians, even
economists, tell him how to run his business. In our ordinary
work-a-day world, few people possess the whole of this cata-
logue of virtues. One man is a splendid organiser, another
a technical genius, a third has a flair for finance. The first
firm will get the goods made in the right quantities at the right
time, but they are a trifle old-fashioned, not exactly what his
customers want. The second firm can turn out a beautiful
piece of work, but you never know when you will get delivery,
and, since art does not wait upon cost, the firm is apt to find
itself in financial difficulties. The third firm is prosperous
enough for the time being. Its costing office is a model of
refined organisation but there are whispers about the quality
of the goods that have been delivered. If we could combine
these three firms, we could use the best qualities of each of the
three and the combined firm would be able to produce a
better article, cheaper, and more profitably than any of the
three original firms could do.

This is exactly what a large firm aims at doing. It divides
the functions of management up into many parts. The actual
form which the organisation takes will, of course, vary with
the particular circumstances of individual firms, and different
products. But certain broad divisions are common to them
all. The Board of Directors determines the policy. The
methods of carrying that policy into effect are the concern of
the managing director and the chief administrative officers.
Financial control, estimating, and costing are separated from
buying and selling on the one side, from manufacturing and
the control of production on the other. The planning
of the detailed organisation of production, the keeping of
the statistics of output and sales, the forecasting of future
sales, and the exploration of possible markets are all likely to
be entrusted to special officers whose sole concern is with

these problems. Transportation, advertising, the main-tenance of machinery and of buildings are likely in most cases to be put in the hands of specialists, with the necessary quali-fications for their particular tasks.

To perform each function, the large firm selects the man who is best fitted for it by aptitude and experience. If a job is divisible into two parts, one requiring comparatively rare and expensive abilities, the other more ordinary and cheaper qualities, a first class man can be employed wholly on the former, a good, steady but unoriginal plodder on the latter. Rare and expensive abilities are not wasted on routine work, routine workers are not asked to make decisions and take responsibilities for which they may be by temperament and training ill-prepared. In a large modern business there is the greatest possible division of labour, not only in production, but also in administration.

The gains from this elaborate division of labour are of two kinds. In the first place special abilities can be used to the full. It is a waste to employ for half his time on clerical work a man who is capable of making important decisions, and who, naturally enough, demands the salary appropriate to such ability. Secondly, the man who is allowed to become a specialist is able to increase his knowledge of the particular task which is assigned to him. The overworked manager who bought the raw materials for his firm, as well as doing a hun-dred other things, might have a flair for buying, but he could not possess half the knowledge of markets which he would have were he the specialist buyer of a large firm. Another small manager may have ideas about the adaptation of machinery to the special needs of the firm, but with fifty other things to do, he could not achieve the expert knowledge which a few years' concentrated study in a large firm will give him. The very large firm enjoys as a rule a further advantage. It is able to buy the most expert accountant, the most skilled designer, the most able organiser. He will be an expensive man, perhaps one of those mysterious £10,000 a year men for whom, we are always told, there is an unsatisfied demand,

and for whose post, and salary, we always imagine ourselves so peculiarly suited. But when he is found, he is nearly always cheap at his price. A man who could reduce by one penny the cost of making a Ford car would be worth over £10,000 a year to the company. It is seldom that the really outstanding expert receives more than a tithe of the difference that he makes to efficiency.

§ 2. **Further Economies of Large Managements.** In addition to these economies of specialisation and division of labour, a large firm can obtain an economy because certain services do not have to be increased in the same ratio as the growth of the firm, or, if increased in the same ratio, are much more efficient. Let us take as an example of this the office concerned with sales forecasting. A firm which is of fairly considerable size is likely to possess such an office. If that firm doubles its size it can secure a more expert, and therefore possibly more expensive, group of economists to take charge of the task; but if the office was reasonably well equipped before, it is unlikely that the expenditure would be doubled. Double the size of that firm again, and there is no appreciable further expenditure in that direction which will yield any further return. Sales forecasting has reached its limit, but the cost of the office per unit of product falls as the firm grows in size.

Can we find any traces of that second force, the Integration of Process, at work on the side of management? Since it applies essentially to mechanical equipment, we should naturally expect it to be less prominent here than in the workshops. But even in the office the machine is rapidly making a place for itself. One of the most important changes of recent years has been the great growth of machine book-keeping. Where before several separate entries were made, a single machine now makes at one typing the invoice for the customer, the order to the department concerned, the record of sales for the statistical department, as well as the records for the ledgers. It adds the total, and keeps a check on all

4—s.c.i.

sales. Where statistical data must be analysed another machine can be employed to sort and classify with certainty and speed. In increasing numbers of cases use is being made of electronic calculating machines. A large, or moderately large, firm has this advantage over firms too small to install and use such equipment profitably.

The economies due to management in a large firm are not limited to increases in the efficiency of management itself. One of the chief tasks of the management of a firm is the organisation and planning of production, so that the worker can proceed without interruption and delay with his own work. If the management of a large firm is more efficient than that of a small firm in this respect, as well as being cheaper, the large firm will possess further advantages over the small. In practice the specialists of the large firm can usually succeed in planning production so that the worker suffers fewer interruptions in his work. His material is brought to him, his finished work taken away. His tools are ground for him, the method of tackling a job worked out for him by experts, jigs are designed and prepared to simplify his task, his machine is kept in good order by a special staff. The work is planned so that he changes over only so often as is absolutely necessary from one task to another; for a change, we have seen, always involves a waste of time while the machine is re-set and the small preliminary difficulties of starting a new job are overcome.

In a small firm, again, where the staff is small, it is a difficult task for the management to assign newcomers to the departments, or to the work to which they are best fitted; in the large firm, where the flow of vacancies is larger, it is easier to secure that at least the best of those who come are assigned at once to the type of work on which they will ultimately be employed. It is possible, also, to afford the expense of a department properly equipped to test the abilities of applicants and to ensure that they possess the physical and mental qualities necessary for success in the department to which they are to go. At later stages, moreover, the large firm can afford the expenses of a training organisation which will equip selected members of its staff to carry greater responsibility.

In these and other ways the large firm is able to secure an efficiency of work which is usually beyond the reach of the small firm. Where economies of this type are available a large firm can afford an administrative staff which, per unit of product, is more expensive than that of the smaller firm. For the higher costs of management are offset by the lower costs of the actual productive departments, due to the efficiency of the management.

§ 3. The Limits to the Gains of Large Management. If all these advantages are to be found for the large firm, why is it that we do not find industries entirely composed of very large firms? The answer is that the very large firm has certain disadvantages, and certain limits, while the small firm has certain advantages of its own. First let us consider the limits of the large firm. We saw in the case of the technical optimum scale that beyond a certain point further division of labour gave little or no further economies. Exactly the same is true in the case of the management and office staff. A certain stage is reached beyond which a further division of labour is either impossible or else unprofitable. There are few offices in which several men, or several women, are not occupied in doing precisely similar work, often concerned with customers whose names belong to different parts of the alphabet. Where this is found in the office of a progressive firm, it may be taken to prove that here at least no economy is to be obtained by specialising each on one part of the work that is being done. Mr. Urwick quoted some years ago a very interesting example of the limits to the profitable division of labour. When the sales office of Rowntree & Co. at York was in process of being reorganised, the extent of the division of labour was actually reduced in order that the correspondence with individual customers and decisions with regard to the granting of credit to customers should be concentrated under a single control. By dealing with a smaller number of customers the clerks concerned could carry in their heads enough knowledge to make constant reference to records unnecessary. By this concentration, it was hoped also to make the work of section heads more varied and more responsible, in order that future executive officers of the Company might be trained by this means. In other cases also it has been found that, beyond a point, further division of labour added little efficiency and, by reducing it to routine, destroyed much of the interest of the work.

§ 4. **The Problem of Co-ordination.** But even if firms ceased to grow where further division of labour ceased to be profitable, and where further integration of processes was impossible, their size would be very great, greater in all probability than we find in most industries to-day. Some other additional explanation would seem to be necessary to account for the multiplicity of firms in most industries. We shall find this explanation in the problem of co-ordination. Every time that a further division of labour is introduced, every time that a job which was previously done by one man or one group of men is divided into two or more parts, the problem of co-ordinating the work of the now separated groups or individuals begins to arise. When the wheel-wright built the cart from shafts to tail-board, no problem of co-ordinating his activities existed. But as soon as the lorry factory takes over these functions, it becomes someone's task to see that the assembly lines are provided with wheels by this department, an engine by that department, a body shell by a third. A new and wholly separate function thus begins to appear. In order that the large firm may be more efficient than the small, the individual parts of the large firm have got to work more efficiently as members of a large firm than as members of a small. A platoon may drill very well as a platoon, but it may not always cover itself with equal glory in battalion drill. A battalion requires officers to co-ordinate the actions of its companies and platoons over and above the platoon commanders.

The battalion has to be fitted into larger organisations, the brigade, the division, and the army. The problem of commanding an army is not simply the sum of the problems of commanding the platoons in it. All sorts of problems of organisation and co-ordination arise because the unit to be controlled is now large instead of small, is out of ear-shot, takes time, space, and forethought to manage. A mistake made by a platoon commander demands only an instantaneous 'As you were!' A mistake by an Army Commander may require days of labour to set right. In just the same way the problem of organising a large firm grows in complication as the firm grows. If the management of a large firm is to be more efficient than that of a small firm, the increase of efficiency due to the division of labour and the employment of specialists must be sufficient to outweigh the cost of the necessary co-ordination, or, as more often happens, the loss of efficiency and flexibility due to the impossibility of perfect co-ordination.

How big a firm can successfully grow will depend upon how it solves this problem of the co-ordinating of separated departments and separated specialists. Those who are expert in the management of large businesses have evolved by trial and error various different forms of organisation which differ in their way as completely as the political forms of adjacent countries differ. The Line or Departmental organisation enables the responsible officers to concentrate their attention on a particular product or process. The problems of the quantities to be produced, the sales of the final products, and, in most cases, the buying of the raw materials, are not the concern of the departmental manager. Within the department some specialisation of the sub-managers, foremen, and clerical staff is possible, but unless the firm is very large, complete specialisation is impossible. In this form of organisation, co-ordination of department with department by a central planning department and a central costing department is necessary. Co-ordination is also necessary, or at least desirable, as regards methods of payment, of wage-fixing, of engagement and dismissal of employees.

To make possible a higher degree of specialisation, the Functional type of organisation has been employed. Where this is in use functional departments are formed which become responsible for one particular function, as contrasted with the one particular product of the Departmental organisation. One department is responsible for all matters concerned with personnel; another is concerned with the maintenance and repair of all machinery; a third with the maintenance and equipment of buildings; a fourth with all transport, internal and external, and so on. The production manager organises production, in most cases with the ordinary system of departments divided according to products, but each of these departments shares the services of the specialist departments as regards all the functions for which they are responsible. By this type of organisation, much more complete co-ordination of the specialist functions is possible, division of labour in these respects can be carried further, experts can be employed to deal with tasks which under the Departmental organisation were the part-time occupation of men whose main training and interest was for other tasks. But though in this way individual problems can be more expertly managed, each department will be invaded by numerous outside experts, decisions affecting his department will be made by others than the head of the department concerned, and the co-ordination of the various authorities within each individual department will be more difficult and demand more diplomacy than in the simpler method of the Departmental organisation.

Yet another type of organisation deserves mention. In this a division of labour is attempted between the work of organising current production and the work of thinking ahead and planning improvements in methods of production and organisation. This type of organisation is commonly known as Line and Staff. The Line is responsible for current production. The Staff's duty is to investigate possible improvements of design, of methods of manufacture and factory

equipment, of distribution, of transport, of internal organisation, of personnel management, and so on. The Line and
Staff method is thus a compromise between the purely Line
organisation, and the completely Functional.

In these various ways attempts are being made to solve the
problems of co-ordination in large businesses. In no department of British industry has progress been so great in the
last twenty-five years as in that of management. The
organisation of factory statistics, the effective utilisation of
available information, the forecasting of markets, and the
timely adjustment of the productive machine to fluctuations
in demand have all been greatly improved. But in many
respects the organisation of large businesses still falls behind
the best practice in the United States.

§ 5. The Advantages of Small Managements. So far we have
considered only the limits to the economies of large units of
management. We have to consider also the particular
advantages which are enjoyed by the managements of small
firms, advantages which tend to disappear as the firm grows
big. We have seen that where managements are big and the
individuals making decisions are numerous, the task of co-
ordinating their actions and decisions grows increasingly
important and difficult. With a small firm, with fewer people
to consult and to persuade, decisions can be reached much
more quickly and easily. Anyone who has ever done business
with committees knows that five people can reach a decision,
fifteen people can be persuaded by a man who has made up
his mind, and twenty-five people are a debating society. It
has been said, and a great deal of experience goes to support
it, that no individual can effectively control more than four
or five subordinate departmental heads. If he attempts to
manage more he must either cause endless delays, or else become no more than a rubber stamp. And so the big firm is
always in danger of becoming a series of wheels within wheels,
an elaborate hierarchy, in which every decision requires the

consulting of this man, the referring to that man, the permission of a third, the agreement of a fourth, so that decisions become endlessly delayed.   Where decisions have to be reached frequently and quickly, such an organisation, unless despotically controlled, may find itself paralysed, and if it is in fact a despotism much of the gain of specialist control must be lost.

The small firm, on the other hand, is more often and more successfully despotic.   The decisions are those, as a rule, of a single individual, made quickly and decisively.   Contrast the making of a decision by a large and a small firm.   A motor car firm, we will suppose, is considering the adoption of a modification to its current model.   The Designer is convinced that it will improve its performance.   The Costing Department has estimated the cost, and determined what change of price is necessary.   The Production Manager is afraid that it will upset all his output plans.   The Sales Department is not sure whether the public will pay the extra price for the slightly improved car.   In some way or other the Board of Directors has to weigh these different considerations in the different experts' minds against one another and reach a decision.   How much simpler is the decision where the same individual is balancing in his mind the gains of the improvement that he has designed, the difficulties and costs which he will meet in incorporating it, and the effects of the modification that he, better than any other, can judge upon the demand for the car. Where an industry requires frequent and immediate decisions of the sort that are not easily reached by a committee, the highly individualist small firm tends to survive and prosper. This is one of the chief reasons why the small firm is strongest in all those industries in which fashion rules, and in which changes of design are constant.   It is strong also in those industries where the conditions of production are so varying that important decisions must be made at frequent intervals, as in building or agriculture.   Where the important decisions are infrequent, and the necessity for a quick decision is less urgent, the large firm can play its part more efficiently.

Besides its advantage in flexibility, the small, usually

privately owned, undertaking enjoys sometimes but not always an advantage in the individual energy of its owner or directors. There are many who will work more efficiently and untiringly for their own hand than for another's. There are many who are better able themselves to make decisions than to persuade others how to make decisions. In the big firm, with its more bureaucratic organisation, the man who can write a memorandum, or explain a problem lucidly, is more valuable than the incoherent, but often more profound and practical individualist. If men will give more of themselves, and get more out of others in a small firm, and if their personality and drive can offset the superior efficiency of the employees of the large firm, then we may find the small firm surviving and flourishing, as it does in many British industries even now. The individualism and self-sufficiency of British industrialists make them at once difficult to co-ordinate, and admirable managers of small firms. To distinguish the gains from the losses is difficult. In those industries in which large scale is technically necessary it is a handicap that we are only gradually eliminating; in those industries in which individual attention to detail is necessary it is often a source of strength. A multiplicity of small firms may be evidence not of industrial backwardness, but of a wealth of managing ability.

§ 6. **The Importance of Individuals.** In these last few pages, forms of organisation, types of businesses, principles of administration have been discussed at length. It would be a mistake not to pay the greatest attention to them. It would be an equal mistake to imagine that a single type of organisation, or a single slogan of administration, is the solution to every business problem. Organisations are no more than frameworks into which real living people have to be fitted. An organisation which would have suited Lord Leverhulme would not in all probability have fitted Andrew Carnegie or Lord Nuffield. In many industries to-day the number of important firms can be counted on one's fingers. Nearly all these firms have one man to whom we can point as the creator of the firm.   Thousands of critics will speak of the 'forces' and the 'principles' and 'the national characteristics' behind the British and the American motor industries, who would not dream of applying these so often meaningless terms to a comparison of the English and Australian cricket teams.   Yet a comparison of Ford and Morris requires no more the obscurity of a pseudo-scientific jargon than a comparison of Hobbs and Bradman and May.   When we talk about the optimum firm in the motor industry, we can of necessity mean little more than the size of firm that Ford and his lieutenants on the one hand, Morris and his men on the other, could successfully manage.   So long as Ford or the likes of Ford were forthcoming the Ford organisation might be for them at least the optimum.   But we must never forget that in this case Ford is the assumption from which we are starting.   The past decade has shown that Fords, without Henry Ford the First, had to find a new organisation.   But what if we had five Fords?   It is possible that though it is more efficient than any smaller organisation, the Ford works has outgrown its strength.   Would our five Fords be better employed together in one firm, or separately in five firms?   We have no means of saying.   The problem of the optimum firm may become the problem familiar to politics, the problem of getting the greatest use out of a limited number of really able men.   The individual firm may be of necessity larger than considerations of maximum efficiency would dictate, but even at the point of lowered efficiency this may remain greater than that of all possible substitutes.

§ 7. **Does Management Set a Limit?**   As to the answer to this question there has been in recent years much dispute.   It may be argued (and I myself would tend to agree) that beyond a point there are no further economies, either technical or managerial, from further division of labour.   On the other hand as size is further increased, there are additional costs per unit of output for co-ordination.   Thus beyond a point the cost of management per unit of output tends to rise.

Whether or not this is true, and—even more important—the sort of size at which these problems are likely to emerge, will depend upon the extent to which it is in fact possible to extend into the sphere of co-ordination itself the principles of the division of labour.   If diminishing returns to the firm are to arise from the existence of the necessity for co-ordination, it must be because more of the other factors of production are of necessity being applied to a limited capacity to co-ordinate.   Why cannot co-ordination itself be increased as required?

To that question those who continue to regard co-ordination as a limited and limiting factor will answer that it is undoubtedly possible to extend co-ordination in some degree by division of labour: that one can so organise a large concern —and particularly a multi-plant concern—that most of the tasks of co-ordination are delegated to plant managers.   But when some of the problems of co-ordination have been solved by delegation in this way, most of the possible gains of larger scale have been surrendered.   The concern has simply become a nexus of moderate-sized plants held together by a common ownership.   This is what many such concerns in fact are.   If, on the other hand, there remains effective central control, with centralisation of the really important decisions of investment, of product-mix (if it is a multi-product firm), of selection of individuals for senior posts, of price policy in a broad sense, the problems of the adequacy or inadequacy of the centralised knowledge on which these decisions are made will remain real problems, and the really essential co-ordinating decisions must be handled and understood by a small group at the centre, which cannot be considerably enlarged without loss of efficiency.

Where such differences of opinion exist it is necessary to judge between them.   My own view is that organisations can be too big and too complex as well as too small and too simple. But I would myself now incline to put the issue in rather more dynamic terms and not in terms of a comparison of a large organisation and a small organisation in static conditions.

The experiences of war-time, as well as those of peace, have shown the very remarkable technical economies of manufacture that can be secured in some industries if very long runs of absolutely unchanged output can be obtained in a very large plant, and if modern tools and equipment can be designed accordingly. If change is not required, I should not be inclined to stress the difficulties of managing the very large resulting concern, so long as it remains engaged in continuous and unvaried production.

On the other hand I would emphasise the danger of ossification of the very large organisation. Mere size makes it in important ways less adaptable to a changing world, and I would put the issue in the more dynamic terms of the probable obsolescence both of the plant and of the product, so that it is in danger of being outstripped by smaller and more adaptable rivals.

This danger of ossification becomes much more serious if one remembers that the concept that apparently underlies much of the more simple presentation of economy theory— the concept of a firm engaged in producing a given standard and unchanging commodity for a given market with equipment the life of which is limited only by wear and tear—is an oversimplified and unrealistic concept which needs to be withdrawn before one can fully understand the complexities of the relation of the firm to its industry in real life. The number of products which go on being turned out in standard unchanging form over a period of twenty years is very small. There are a very few examples in the textile industries. There are a few examples in other trades, particularly of semi-finished products. But in a great many industries the ordinary life cycle of a design or a product is usually limited to ten years and is often under five years, and more often than not it is less than that of the machinery used to produce it. One of the fundamental problems facing a manufacturer in many industries is the choice between acquiring special tooling and equipment that will turn out to-day's product with minimum cost and using more versatile methods and equipment which will reduce the cost of turning over to the succeeding design, and reduce also his loss if to-day's design becomes obsolete earlier than had been expected.

The problem of managements is thus in practice a dynamic problem of constant manœuvre and adjustment to a world of changing tastes, changing relative costs of plant and operative labour, of raw materials and their substitutes, of changing techniques, where one needs to be abreast without incurring the penalties of beating the gun by buying experimental equipment before its makers have 'got the bugs out of it.' It is in this world of manœuvre that the very large and the very inflexible organisation, heavily committed to last year's techniques and last year's products, may be outstripped by the well-managed smaller firm.

Thus set in these rather more dynamic terms, I would still think that problems of management in certain contexts set an upper limit to the optimum size of the closely integrated productive unit. But that size may be considerably larger than is required on any technical grounds in most industries to-day. Some economists have written in terms of progressively falling costs ultimately turning into progressively rising costs when optimum size is past: what has now come to be called the U-shaped cost curve. That may represent the actual state of affairs in some industries, though real-life cost curves never have the steepness either of fall or of rise which some economic theorists and their block-makers delight in depicting. But there is evidence to support the view that the greater part of the technical economies of scale are secured in some industries by relatively modest size; on the other hand, any serious diseconomies of size emerge only after fairly considerable size has been reached. In such cases there may be a plateau of almost constant costs covering a fairly wide range of sizes within which the majority of firms in the industry will be found to lie. Both on practical and theoretical grounds there is much to be said for such a possibility. There are a number of industries in which firms of considerably different size appear to survive in effective competition with each other.

CHAPTER IV

THE OPTIMUM FINANCIAL UNIT

§ 1. The Borrowing Powers of Firms. The cost of production of a firm and its size will depend not only upon the technique of manufacture, and upon the efficiency of management and sales, but also upon the ability of the firm to borrow the capital necessary for its activities. If opportunities for borrowing depend in any sense upon size, the problems of finance will influence the optimum scale of production. In practice, we find that the task of raising capital exerts important influences both upon the size and upon the structure of firms. It does this in two ways; firstly through the rates at which firms can borrow, secondly through the amounts that firms of different types of organisation can borrow at any given rate. A firm in one set of circumstances may be able to borrow small amounts at a comparatively favourable rate, another firm in another set of circumstances may be able to borrow small amounts at a less favourable rate, but larger amounts at a more favourable rate than the first firm. The policy and structure of the firm may be determined by its choice between these two alternatives.

Let us start by considering the limits set by the amounts which firms can borrow. Until little more than a hundred years ago, restrictions were imposed upon the association of individuals to form companies for purposes of trade, and the company form of organisation, apart from a few important exceptions, was rare. The abolition of these restrictions and the additional grant of limited liability have greatly changed the typical form of industry. Where a large capital is necessary, the joint stock company with limited liability has become common. The company form of organisation enables the promoters or controllers of business to pass on to the general public any part of the task of financing a business which they do not themselves wish to undertake. The shareholders of a company perform two separate functions. They provide the capital and they run the risks, the risks either of losing their money or of achieving wealth. The promoters of the company may hand over the performance of both these functions to the general public, themselves becoming no more than leading shareholders or even withdrawing entirely, or they may retain in their own hands most of the risks and opportunities, and apply to the public only for the provision of capital at fixed, or virtually fixed, rates of interest.

The ordinary investor is content as a rule to provide capital more cheaply than those who are in a position to promote and control businesses. The latter expect a higher return for their activities of enterprise and the bearing of the initial risks than will be secured by a shareholder in a mature and stable undertaking. The passing on to the general public of the task of providing capital makes possible also the employment of large amounts of saving which might otherwise be wasted. Stocks and shares are issued, which may be quickly realised by sale on the Stock Exchange. This possibility will enable those who have savings available for a comparatively short period to put them at the disposal of industry. These many short strands of savings may be spun together into a continuous thread of constantly available resources.

§ 2. **Methods and Rates of Growth.** The financial structure of firms is influenced largely by one aspect of the technical methods of the particular industry. In some industries, firms must start at almost their full stature, in other industries they normally start small and grow up to their full stature. Thus a railway company, a canal company, a cable company, an electricity supply company, must start with almost its full equipment of capital in order that it shall provide any service at all. A publisher, a radio or plastics firm, an hotel, on the other hand, may start with an insignificant capital, and expand gradually as it finds customers. The former type of industry requires to be joint stock, because the initial capital is too large for one person to supply. The latter may, and usually does, start as an individual enterprise and grows later, if at all, into a joint stock company. It is probably for this reason that we find that in the cotton industry the joint stock type of organisation predominates on the spinning side of the trade, where no gradual change of the scale of operations is possible after the initial investment, while it is far less common on the weaving side, where growth is for technical reasons far more simple. The moment at which a firm will find it desirable to change its financial structure will depend mainly on the profits which it is earning. Industry in Great Britain relies chiefly upon profits as a source of capital. We have no separate figures for manufacturing industry, but companies of all sorts, manufacturing and trading, saved in 1956 more than the whole of their gross investment in fixed capital and in increased stocks.

The normal method of obtaining capital, that is to say, is to divide between shareholders less than the whole of the profits made in any year. But to grow in this manner means that a financial limit is set upon the rate of expansion. To-day, with very heavy taxation of profits, the limit set on expansion is a more severe one than that to which firms were subjected before the war. There is no reason to think that the most efficient rate of growth is that set by the available profits either in the period before the war, or at the present moment. As to what is the maximum efficient rate, individuals in the same industry appear to hold widely divergent views. A firm, it must be remembered, is an organism in itself. Its parts depend upon each other. Smooth working arises, we have seen, from the most perfect co-ordination of many individuals. A too rapid expansion will introduce so many disharmonious elements that efficiency will be destroyed. In some industries, a rate of growth greater than some 10 per cent per annum appears to lead to confusion; in other industries, a firm would seem able to multiply its output several times in a year without detriment. The most efficient rate of growth would appear to be lower in those industries where a high degree of planning and co-ordination is necessary, higher in those where the technical processes of production are fairly straightforward, and the different departments not closely interdependent.

§ 3. **The Influence of Forms of Organisation upon Enterprise.** Where the efficient rate of growth is higher than can be secured by expansion out of profits, recourse must be had to one or other of the methods of raising capital from the public. So long as the firm is owned and run by a single individual, he may regard the protection of limited liability as unnecessary. For it serves only to protect any property which he possesses outside his business, and if this property is small, he may regard the costs of turning his firm into a company as unjustified. A very large part of British industry and commerce is still carried on by ordinary firms enjoying no advantage of limited liability. If, however, he wishes to expand faster than his savings permit, and to give the undertaking an existence independent of the lives of its owners, he must turn it into a private or public company. A private company is limited to fifty members. There are restrictions to the right to transfer shares. It may not appeal to the general public to subscribe either for shares or debentures. If more funds are required than can be secured even by a private company, it will become necessary to set up a public company. But this involves at least a formal compliance with the regulations governing the establishment of public companies. The company must have two or more directors, it must publish its accounts, it must hold an annual meeting at which the directors may be held accountable to the public for their stewardship. The public will judge their success or failure largely by the dividends which they distribute if the public holds the ordinary shares, by the dividends which they do not distribute if the public holds only debentures.

There are many leaders of business to-day, particularly in those industries where initiative and a willingness to take risks

5—S.C.I.

are important, who hold the view that the public company type of organisation, which makes them responsible in part at least to others, is a cramping influence upon their enterprise, that checks and safeguards are necessary which, apart from shareholders, they would have regarded as superfluous, that pressure will be put upon them to do things which in the long run they do not consider wise, that the autocracy which is the foundation of their efficiency will be confined and limited.   If this view is justified, then in certain cases a firm must choose between greater immediate efficiency and a higher rate of growth.   Clearly the advantage will not always be found on the one side or the other, but it is important to remember that it is precisely during a period of growth that initiative and enterprise and the power of subordinating immediate gains to a longer advantage are most vital.   Nor is rapidity of growth always the surest criterion of ultimate success.   If a bull calf and an elephant calf enter the world at the same time, the more quickly maturing bull calf will, after a year or so, be bigger than the still infant elephant, but the bull calf has exhausted its power of further growth, the elephant will soon overtake it again.   In much the same way, rapid growth which sterilises the initiative and efficiency which will make it possible in the long run to produce more cheaply than rivals, and so secure their market, may stunt a firm rather than stimulate it.

This conflict between freedom and capital is not universal. There are many men who are unaffected by a responsibility to shareholders, who can command and mould a firm, whatever its theoretical organisation, into the forms which fit their own genius.   There are others, like Ford the First, who regard any dependence upon money power with abhorrence.   Complete independence is, however, seldom possible. It is a proper function of the banking system to provide a part of the working capital of industry.   In this country, it has been common for firms to provide their own fixed capital, the buildings and machines that they use, out of the funds that they have raised from themselves or their shareholders.   For circulating capital, the materials and the wages bills, they have relied upon the banks. A certain number of old-fashioned firms have always preferred to be self-sufficient not only as regards fixed, but also as regards circulating capital. In some other countries, and in particular in Germany, the banks have gone further in the direction of supplying the fixed capital of industry than have the banks of this country hitherto. But in recent years, the heavy taxation on the one side, the growth of insurance on the other, have led to a concentration of new savings in other hands than those of the controllers of business. It is important, therefore, that the channels for the transmission of this saving to those who can best use it should be as broad and as open as possible, and that, so far as is possible, the act of borrowing should not operate to restrict the initiative of those who can make best use of the savings.

There is another facet to this problem which deserves a moment's attention. It has been argued in the last paragraph that the small firm, the partnership, or the private company, has opportunities of freedom which a public joint stock company may not enjoy, and that the enterprise and efficiency of management may be greater. In many cases that is true. But it is not always that managing ability and the ownership of capital are combined. The public joint stock company has an advantage of its own in that it is a means of separating the functions of providing capital and of controlling it, and where it calls to its aid men of first-rate ability who do not possess capital to compete with men of second-rate ability whose main qualification for the control of a business is that they were born rich, the public company, whether or not it is the ideally best organisation, may be the practically more successful. Thus public companies can recruit as their leaders, as has happened recently, men who have already made their marks in the civil service, in the armed forces or in politics. Such a man could build up a firm of his own only after a considerable time, if at all. This gives a considerable advantage to the public company, but it would be a mistake to exaggerate it. Many of the most successful British businesses have been private companies. They have been able to call to their aid men of first-rate ability in the higher subordinate positions, so that in this respect the public company enjoys little superiority. Nor has the lack of capital proved an insuperable handicap in those industries in which growth is possible. Of the great businesses of the private company type, the most notable have been built up in one generation by men who started with nothing.

§ **4. The Advantages of the Large Financial Unit.** So much for the effects of the ease or difficulty in different conditions of borrowing so much as a firm may require. We have also to consider the obverse side of what is ultimately the same problem, the difference of the rates at which large and small firms can borrow. In general, the large firm possesses, of course, an advantage. Its name is better known to the investing public, its standing can be more easily ascertained. A large firm may be able to borrow more than its present circumstances warrant, while a small firm of better real standing may go short. The greater ease with which large firms can borrow money may be one factor leading to the vertical integration of large undertakings, or the absence of vertical disintegration where we should have expected it. The large firm may be able to borrow so much more easily and cheaply the funds required to exploit a new source of raw materials, or to take advantage of new processes of manufacture of some subsidiary product, that though it may be technically less well fitted to control these further processes, there may be economies to be secured by it doing so.

The advantage which a large firm possesses in this way, combined with the growing size of efficient units in many industries, is making the task of growing up to the optimum scale more and more difficult. Its financial structure has given the joint stock company a continuity of life greater than that of the individuals who control it. In the nineteenth century, firms grew, matured, and declined. The firms in an industry, in Marshall's famous simile, resembled the trees of

the forest.   Some were at their full height, others growing towards it, others were decaying.   In this century the firm's
cycle of life is far less pronounced.   A firm is built up, usually
as a private company, it reaches maturity, it declines, but it
does not die.   It is reorganised, new blood is brought in, and
the firm may quickly return to the strength of its maturity.   In
some industries, mostly the younger industries, radio, gramophones, electrical goods and electronics, new firms spring up
frequently.   A number survive the diseases of childhood, and
grow to the size of the largest.   But in the older industries the
new firms are rare.   The minimum efficient technical size,
even in the first stages, is too large.   Growth is impossible or
too slow, and capital can be better applied to the re-equipment
of existing undertakings.   In such industries, since the risks
of a new enterprise must be great, the influences of finance lie
on the side of the large firm, and on the side of stability rather
than of change.

§ 5. Does Finance Set a Limit?   If one were concerned solely
with the problems of relative costs of production at different
sizes in a static world, it is to be doubted whether considerations of finance would make a very great difference.   So far as
they did make a difference, finance would be likely to be yet
another factor giving advantage to the big firm, or to the firm
that had got a start as compared with its smaller competitor.
The very small firm, it is true, when it can draw on family
sources of finance, may have a special advantage of its own.
But with heavier death duties and heavier taxation that particular advantage tends to be more limited, and to disappear
before a firm reaches considerable size.

   If, however, one is looking at the problem more dynamically
and is anxious to answer the question why in the real world
all production is not in the hands of a few giants, one is driven
back on to the problems of the rates at which firms can grow
and on to the other factors besides mere size that can make
very great differences to the efficiency and costs of firms, the
personal efficiency of the top management, the whole climate

and tempo of work of the firm. The size of any young firm which is advancing in competition with older firms is largely determined by the capital available to it. The growth of the large firm is often dictated almost equally by the extent to which it can either finance its own further growth or borrow from the market. In some degree the big firm may provide its own financial limitation, judging that great investment would involve increasing risks, or that resources invested in some quite different form of development would bring a greater return in a world of imperfect markets. If, therefore, we are looking for an explanation of the actual size of firms in the real and constantly changing world, the limits of finance are probably as important as any others we may find.

CHAPTER V

THE OPTIMUM MARKETING UNIT

§ **1. The Scope of Marketing Efficiency.** Our next task is to examine the effects of the twin problems of buying and selling upon the optimum firm and the structure of industry. It is important always to remember what a large part these two play in the total expenditure of a firm. The costs of raw material vary, of course, very greatly from industry to industry. A jeweller's materials will play a larger part in the finished price than a baker's, but in each case it is considerable. Of the cost of a loaf of bread, about three-fifths is the cost of the flour. About half of the costs of an engineering firm may be represented by material costs. Of the cost of spinning American cotton yarns, about three-quarters is the cost of the materials. In the case of chemicals or detergents raw material costs may amount to four-fifths of total costs. It is evident then that efficient buying may make as much difference to final profits as efficient manufacturing.

If we turn to the side of selling costs, including in these both the entire sales and advertising costs of the manufacturer and the margins of gross profit of retailers and intermediaries, there are many products for which they amount to 40 per cent or more of the final price, and hardly any for which they are less than 20 per cent. This figure measures, of course, not only the profits which go to the middleman, but his whole expenditure also on the wages, buildings, equipment, and organisation necessary to bring the goods to market. He and his assistants are providing a useful service to us as consumers, and they require to be paid for it. But it can be readily seen that economies fully as large as any in the process of manufacture can be achieved in the subsequent marketing of the goods.

§ 2. The Economies of Large Scale Buying.   Let us first consider the advantages and disadvantages of large scale buying.
At first sight the advantages appear to preponderate.   The
large firm can buy large amounts of raw materials as a single
order.   The firm that produces the raw materials can increase
its output of the particular material required, and can afford
to sell it more cheaply.   A firm that can buy special steels
fifty tons at a time can always get a better price than a firm
which orders the same steel in fifty hundredweight lots. Moreover, where a single consumer is very large in relation to the
whole market for a certain material, the producer cannot so
lightly allow the order to pass him by.   He will be driven,
if there is competition, to quote his lowest price rather than the
take-it-or-leave-it price which he may successfully quote to
other smaller undertakings.   The large firm, particularly if
it is one of few large firms, is then in a stronger bargaining
position as against its suppliers than the small firm.   The
large firm possesses a further advantage; because it is large,
it can afford expert buyers, backed up by all the resources of
scientific knowledge and equipment.   Buying specifications
may be more detailed.   The tests to which the materials will
be put may be more rigid, so that less work is spoiled by faulty
material, and the quality of the final product is higher and
more uniform, so that by its reputation it can command a
higher price.

So far the advantages have lain entirely on the side of large
scale buying, but there are two important considerations
which weigh upon the other side.   Firstly, the greatest expert
is fallible, and he may lead the whole buying staff of a large
firm into error.   During the war, it sometimes happened that
the same individuals who had purchased materials for private
industry in times of peace, found themselves appointed as a
board to buy on behalf of the Government.   Though in peace
time they would have formed independent views, some antici-

pating a rise of price, some a fall, so that their errors cancelled out and their total action was appropriate to the circumstances, in war time they were often persuaded by the arguments or the insistence of some one individual into taking a collective view which was widely wrong. In much the same way, we may doubt whether the judgment of the experts of a single very large firm is more accurate than the sum of the judgments of the many buyers of smaller firms.

But this would not in itself be a handicap to the large firm if it suffered no further difficulty, for we have to compare the error of the large firm not with the sum of the cancelling errors of the smaller firms, but with the error to which any individual smaller firm would be liable, whether by buying in excess or deficiency at current prices. The very large firm, however, suffers from a second disadvantage. The small firm, when it makes an error, can usually redeem it by buying or selling its deficiencies or surpluses on the open market; but where one firm is so large as to form a preponderating part of the whole market, it may be impossible for it to correct an initial error without so affecting market prices that its mistakes can be only in small measure retrieved. We have seen from time to time examples of very large undertakings entering into long-period contracts for raw materials which have handicapped them heavily in competition with other technically less efficient producers.

Our argument would suggest, then, that while better terms can be secured for large orders, a firm obtains very little added advantage and great added responsibility by growing so large that it is, within a given country, almost the sole user of certain of its raw materials. The less fluctuating and subject to climatic variations are the conditions of output of the raw material, the less liable are errors of judgment to outweigh economies of large scale buying. And in those cases where raw materials must be produced to some particular specification to meet the requirements of a single firm, the greater is the advantage of the large scale production of these special materials, the greater will be the gain to the firm which can

buy upon a large scale. But it is interesting to find that at
least one large firm is convinced that it buys most cheaply and
diminishes its risks if it decentralises the buying and makes
each plant manager responsible for his own buying.

§ 3. **Sales Costs and a Difficulty of Analysis.** We must now
turn to consider the effects of the selling of goods upon the
optimum size of the firm, and see how far a large firm has an
advantage, and how far any advantages that it enjoys are
likely to be offset by countervailing disadvantages. Unfortunately, we encounter almost at once a difficulty of analysis.
The cost of selling is only in part, and in certain conditions, a
cost of production. At other times and in other conditions, it
is a cost not of producing but of growing. For once the
market has been won, it can be retained at a lower selling cost
than is necessary to secure it initially. We have, then, two
quite distinct questions to which we must give an answer.
First, is a larger firm more efficient than a smaller firm?
Second, will it pay to grow from being smaller to being larger?
The high cost of selling may be, paradoxically, at the same
time a source of economy, making the already large firm
more efficient than the smaller firm, and a cost of growth
which makes it unprofitable for the small firm to grow up to
its most efficient size. We shall have to consider in a later
chapter how the costs of growth may be reduced by amalgamation and combination, rather than direct expansion, and
the reactions of this upon industrial organisation and structure. For the moment, I shall defer the consideration of
those selling costs which are properly a cost of growth, and
assume that we can distinguish the two costs sufficiently to
assign some part to growth, the remainder to routine selling.
In practice, of course, such distinction is difficult. The fact
that another firm is attempting to grow may involve an existing firm in added defensive expenditure, and that will in turn
increase the routine costs as well as the growing costs of the
growing firm. Whito advertises more, Brighto retaliates;
Whito increases its expenditure again, and so it goes on with-

out end. The poor gullible public gets more acres of paper and fewer ounces of detergent for every pound that it spends.

Though advertising, purely for industrial warfare, is sometimes wasteful, it is at other times a necessary and desirable expenditure. Sometimes it serves the purpose of drawing our attention to improvements of existing articles. A better safety razor, a faster or more economical motor car, a more luxurious arm-chair is available, and we ought to know it. At other times, it tells us of new articles, or unrealised needs. New books, new cameras, new domestic gadgets, or labour-saving devices, which have just been invented to make life more simple, or possibly more complicated, must be brought to our attention. At other times again, some article that we already know and possibly use has been made cheaper, and if we are to spend our income so that it brings us in the most satisfaction, we must know the changed price and take it into account. In all these ways, advertising may be valuable and productive.

It is economical also where it can cajole buyers into increased standardisation of their wants. If I buy a standard Morris car, I not only enjoy myself the advantage of the large scale on which it is produced, but I also help, by adding my order to the thousands of existing orders, to increase the scale of its output, and thus probably make it cheaper for others. If I refuse to buy the standard car, and buy a car turned out by a little manufacturer, I help him, it is true, but I damage by my decision all the purchasers of Morris cars. If the one car is really as good as the other, and if the total cost of turning out all the cars at Cowley, plus the cost of inducing people to buy nothing but Morrises, is less than the total cost of manufacturing both the Morris cars on the smaller scale and the rival cars, then everyone is better off than before, and the expenditure on advertising is beneficial.

Though it may be true that in some few such cases advertisement is to be regarded as desirable, in very many cases it is purely wasteful. But we must always remember that we have no one to blame for that except ourselves. If it were not true that a shilling spent on advertising brought in more orders

than a shilling taken off the price of the goods, manufacturers
presumably would not advertise.   If we want more goods and
less paper, then the remedy is in our own hands.   We must
buy the goods of the manufacturers who do not waste money
on advertising, and say to ourselves, 'I will never buy A's petrol,
B's tyres, C's cigarettes,' whenever we pass the familiar hoard-
ings.   But in the meantime, being lazy or gullible, we buy the
goods of the manufacturer who shrieks the loudest, and by so
doing we place a great advantage in the hands of the large
firm, for wholesale advertising is an expensive business.

§ 4. The Economies of Large Scale Selling.   For large scale
selling a large firm has certain advantages, but large scale
selling (selling, that is, to a large number of buyers) does not
necessarily entail large scale production.   Some firms produce
upon a large scale and sell upon a small scale.   Others produce upon a small scale, and sell upon a large scale.   Others
again both produce and sell on the same scale, large or small.
Thus manufacturers of railway materials or of military equipment may manufacture upon the largest scale, but since their
customers are few, they need to sell only upon a small scale.
The village baker, on the other hand, may manufacture on a
small scale, but he sells to far more customers than does the
largest manufacturer of machine guns.   Motor manufacturers,
boot and shoe manufacturers, the makers of all those things
which the final customer selects for himself, must sell on a
large scale.   Where the scale of selling is small, an elaborate
sales organisation is seldom necessary, and the saving from
using more fully what organisation there is, will have but little
effect upon the optimum scale as a whole.   But where a large
number of sales have to be made, and the sales costs are
responsible for a large proportion of the final price, there will
be a considerable gain if the quantity of goods to be sold is
large; travellers and salesmen will be able to work nearer to
their full capacity, and their capacity for making sales is
enormous.   To book a large order is not much more laborious
than to book a small order.   The traveller of the large firm,

who books an order four times as large as the traveller of the small firm, does not incur four times his costs. If two firms, each of which has a market extending all over the country, are amalgamated to form one large firm, it will seldom be necessary to maintain the whole of the duplicated sales staffs.

There are other obvious advantages to be secured by the manufacturer who can market on a large scale. Since stocks must always include a certain minimum of each line, the larger sales can often be carried through with relatively smaller stocks, involving smaller interest charges; this will imply a quicker turnover and fresher stocks. But the stocks of the large manufacturer are likely to be larger than those of the small manufacturer in comparison with the maximum orders of wholesalers and retailers, and he can often fill emergency orders from stock when a smaller manufacturer would require time to turn out the goods. A large manufacturer or a large merchant can afford to carry a larger variety of stocks, and attract customers by the wider range of choice that is offered. It is evident then that the large firm enjoys on the side of sales a preponderating advantage over the small firm. The advantage will be still greater where it is necessary to maintain sales organisations not only throughout this country, but also in foreign markets. Few even of the largest firms can maintain a complete sales organisation devoted solely to their interests in all the countries in which their goods might be marketed.

§ 5. **Vertical Disintegration in Selling.** In the case of single technical processes that required large scale, we found that they were taken over by specialist organisations, or specialist firms. Is this done also in the buying and selling? In some cases it is; in the cotton industry, the small producer has been able to obtain almost all of the economies of a large firm in this respect. The cotton market at Liverpool enables him to buy his cotton with the same advantage as the large firm. The yarn market enables him to sell his yarn. If he is a manufacturer, he can buy yarn, weave it, and sell it in the market for cloth. If his goods are for export, they can be handled by a large exporting house which specialises in the market for which he produces. Similar organisations exist in the woollen trade. Large merchant houses give orders to small manufacturers. The manufacturer is able to concentrate upon the task of producing the goods without having to concern himself with the problem of marketing, which is the function of the wholesale house. Each in its own way is as the result of vertical disintegration upon a scale which, if not the optimum, is at least well adapted to the functions to be performed.

For agricultural products similar large marketing organisations exist. In this case, though the free market operates to assist the small producer to secure a better price than he could unaided, and relieves him of the task of marketing, it has been a matter of fairly general complaint that the small producer, because he offers very small parcels, gets a lower price than the large producer and the foreign importer. This is, to some extent at least, inevitable. Where there is reason to suspect that the cause is relative bargaining strength as well as the additional trouble and cost of dealing in small and usually imperfectly graded parcels, some remedy can often be secured by the substitution of co-operative handling for handling by middlemen. This solution has been most successful in Canada, in Ireland, and in Denmark. We have relied to a greater extent on marketing boards with a governmental or semi-governmental status.

In some cases then the small producer is able to escape from the disadvantages which belong to smallness by throwing the task of selling or of buying on to a larger organisation; but such an escape depends upon the standardisation of the product. Where the product is standardised and can be graded, and it is no matter of concern to the original producer whether his product is mixed with other producers' goods or marketed separately, an organised market, or a system of marketing through large wholesale merchants, is suitable to the trade; but where the goods are specialist goods, branded and distinguished by the manufacturer, and sold in competition of quality against the goods of other rival producers, an organised market and the large scale middleman system are less suitable. From the manufacturer's point of view, the motor agent who handles five or six makes of cars is a less satisfactory representative than one who confines himself to a single make. Ford for this reason has usually insisted that local agents shall handle no other type of car. Other manufacturers seek to attach individual retailers to their interests by giving an exclusive agency for their goods to one of a number of retailers in a local market. Thus the agency of the Raleigh cycle has usually been in this sense an exclusive one. Many of these types of exclusive agency have been reconsidered in the past few years in the light of recent legislation designed to discourage monopoly.

Most manufacturers of branded goods prefer to market their own goods so far as the wholesale stage is concerned, because by doing so they can push their own goods in competition of quality at least so far as the retailer, and assist the latter in the further stage of pressing their goods on the final consumer. The chocolate firms, for instance, distribute to all except the smallest retailers direct. The tobacco firms do likewise. Other firms extend their sales organisation even into the retail market. Boots in the druggist trade, Freeman, Hardy & Willis in the boot trade, Montague Burton in the clothing trade provide familiar examples of this. In many cases, however, the advantages of large scale efficient marketing are held to outweigh the disadvantages and difficulties due to rival products being handled by the same firm. Many instances can be found of goods which are competitively marketed by the producers in the home market, but marketed by a common organisation in the foreign market.

In other cases individual firms market their own goods, because the goods are insufficiently standardised to be marketed by intermediaries; engineering and electrical firms, for instance, must have their own representatives and deal direct with their customers, and a large firm which can maintain offices in the chief capitals and ports abroad is able to secure a considerable advantage over the smaller firms. But in very many cases where unstandardised goods have to be marketed, tradition has established the practice of an approach by the customer to the producer. The customer announces his requirements and asks for tenders, either publicly in the press or by direct invitation to the most suitable firms. This is the normal method of marketing in the building trades, for public works, for such part of the structural and engineering work of railway companies as they do not undertake directly themselves, for ship-building, for large electrical installations, and in many other cases where the product to be sold is large and incapable of complete standardisation. It is particularly common in all those instances where the function of designing the product is divorced from that of producing it, so that the customer or his representative lays down the specification to which competing firms must comply, and competition is therefore almost entirely upon a basis of price.

§ 6. **Common Marketing Economies.** There remains to be considered another aspect of the reactions of marketing upon the forms of industrial structure; that which we may call the effect of common marketing economies. In any district, there is a limited market for any one commodity. The limit is set by the amount of money which the population of the district is willing, or can be persuaded, to spend on the commodity in question. Where the population is large and dense, a high degree of specialisation of the final marketing unit, the shop, is possible. In London, shops are more specialised than they are in Cambridge, in Cambridge more so than they are in the villages round about; but even in the most densely populated areas there are few shops to be found which are specialised to the extent of selling only a single brand of a single commodity. London is probably alone in possessing a shop dedicated exclusively to the sale of harps. For the local market, a single commodity is not sufficient to maintain a complete specialised marketing organisation. If an efficient scale of marketing is to be secured, many commodities must be marketed together. The number of different commodities which will be marketed together will depend first upon the size of the local market, and secondly on the type of marketing organisation.

The village shop at one end of the scale, and Selfridge's at the other, are all-sufficient in their respective markets. Between these two limits we find the ordinary shop, corresponding in its organisation to the small factory, a single department closely under the owner's eye, owing its success generally to the energy and efficiency of a single man, marketing a group of commodities which by tradition have come to be regarded as groceries, or millinery, or stationery, but having in many cases no necessary common origin or channel of supply. Just as it would be impossible in most districts to have a single shop which sold nothing but drawing pins, so in a less degree it would be impossible to have a sales organisation connecting the manufacturer and the retailer which handled nothing but drawing pins. In the large cities, such an organisation might be feasible, but in country districts, a very large proportion of the traveller's time is occupied in travelling; when he reaches a customer, only an insignificant addition to his expenses or delay to his other work would be caused by offering several different commodities for sale at the same time. In these circumstances, it may be to the advantage of a manufacturer who is maintaining a sales organisation which, by reason of the limitation of the market, is not working to its full capacity, to increase the range of his products, and to market them all through the single organisation.

We therefore find many examples of branded goods in which the brand applies rather to a range of commodities conveniently manufactured and sold together, but satisfying different wants, than to a single commodity. The reputation of one line is employed to increase the sales of another line. The manufacturer expects to obtain greater economies by employing his sales organisation more fully than by manufacturing a single commodity on a somewhat larger scale. He secures the advantages of a large scale management in his factory by combining under one roof the manufacture of several commodities. If the technical gains of specialised production are small, and the extra costs of creating additional demand by salesmanship and advertising are great, the firm that produces a considerable range of similar goods which can be sold through the same salesmen to the same retailers is likely to have an advantage over the firm which concentrates upon a single line of goods.

§ 7. **Marketing Costs and the Optimum Firm.** Any general statement about the effects of marketing upon optimum size is obviously impossible. We can say first that when goods are sufficiently standardised to be dealt in by an organised market, a small producer can as a rule market his goods economically, and the subsequent stages of distribution are effected by firms on a scale adapted to the work they are doing. In other cases where goods are less standardised, but not sold by name and trade mark, wholesale firms on a large scale can distribute goods produced by small producers without loss to the small producer. In trades in which branded goods are common, the producer must as a rule maintain his own sales and distributing organisation. Since a sales organisation can sell larger amounts, and reduce its failures to make any sale, without proportionate increases in cost, a large firm, once it is established, will save on the cost of sales, and it may therefore be to the advantage of a firm to be larger than the size dictated either by technical considerations or considerations of management other than that concerned with sales.

But though a firm, by being larger, might secure these economies, it will not always be profitable to grow sufficiently to secure them. For growth requires, as a rule, an increase of expenditure upon sales organisation and upon marketing, and an expenditure which increases the more rapidly, the more rapidly the firm attempts to grow, so that additional units of product become for the time being more expensive to bring to market. The increasing costs of sales are therefore a limit to growth which may operate even before the optimum technical and managerial scale has been reached. The potential economy can be secured, and the cost of competitive growth escaped, only by some voluntary association in all those cases where, because of differences of quality and the difficulties of accurately estimating quality, the market is to some degree imperfect.   There is reason to think that competition alone will not in these cases bring about the establishment of optimum firms.

It is at once apparent that a change in the methods of marketing which prevail in an industry will have a profound effect upon the size of the optimum firm in that industry. If a firm in an industry which has hitherto depended either upon an organised market, or upon specialist merchant firms, is compelled by a change of circumstances to market its own goods, the optimum size of the firm is likely to be increased. This is exactly what has happened in many British industries. Before 1914 British goods, particularly in the textile trades, were handled by large merchant firms, sometimes of British nationality, often, in the export markets, of the nationality of the importing country.   These merchants were concerned only with making the greatest possible gains for themselves by buying in the cheapest market for sales in their own market. At that time the British goods were, as a rule, the cheapest, and such competition as existed was between individual British firms.   But in recent years, a great change has taken place.   Many of the merchant houses were so crippled by the slump of 1921 that they have changed in character.   Instead of being merchant houses giving firm orders, and themselves carrying stocks and running risks, they have become agents for the producers, requiring the producer to carry the stocks and to run the risks of the price fluctuations of manufactured stocks.   In some trades the merchant has almost entirely disappeared, and the manufacturer now deals directly with the buyer of the retail firm.   Moreover, where a merchant house has continued to perform its old functions, it is not concerned with pushing the goods of a given producer, or of all producers of a given nationality; it is not prepared to make an immediate loss in order that the goods of producers of a given nationality may capture or recapture a market in which later a profitable goodwill may be established.   The merchant house has comparatively little plant standing idle.   It prefers to accept a smaller trade, provided it does not lose its own share, rather than risk losses by reducing margins in the hope of expanding the trade.

In these several ways there has arisen a conflict of interest between producer and merchant, which was formerly of less importance.   This conflict, combined with the common tendency of producers in times of intense competition to attempt to brand their goods and maintain the demand for them by attaching to them a special reputation for quality, has led to much discussion, for example in the cotton industry, of the continued advantages of dividing sectionally the whole industry, and entrusting special functions to special firms. It is suggested that much larger units might achieve appreciable economies by standardising certain types of cloth, creating a reputation for those cloths, and marketing them by agencies devoted entirely to them.

We have seen in this chapter that the necessity of buying raw materials and selling the finished product requires an organisation which can operate with increasing efficiency almost to the largest possible scale.   Just as a large machine requires a firm large enough to keep it running to its full capacity, so an irreducible sales or buying organisation requires a large undertaking in order that its cost per unit of output may be at a minimum.   There is good reason for thinking that many industries, where by the nature of the product a firm must market its own produce through a sales organisation, will continue to yield economies with further expansion after all the technical economies have been secured, and after the limits of efficient management are approached. Where this is the case, the sales optimum will tend to set a lower limit to the size of the optimum firm.

But though a larger firm may, when it has reached its full scale of production, have a lower cost of producing goods and bringing them to market, it does not follow that a firm will immediately or automatically expand to this larger scale in the ordinary conditions of an imperfect market. For the costs of growth must be set against the gains to be expected from being on a larger scale, and growth will take place only if the gains exceed the costs.

CHAPTER VI

THE INFLUENCE OF RISKS AND FLUCTUATIONS

§ 1. The Effects of Risk and Fluctuations. We have next to consider the effects upon the size of the optimum firm of the existence of risks and changes of demand. Variations of demand may be of four different types. The change may be a permanent one, due to a decline in the popularity of some particular article, owing to the growth either of direct substitutes or of alternative ways of satisfying the same ultimate demand. The change may be a cyclical change, a decline of demand, that is, which is due to a temporary general decline in the power of the community to purchase goods. The change may be a seasonal one, since the particular commodity satisfies needs which arise, or can be met, only at certain times of year. The change, lastly, may be wholly erratic, and due to the failure of individual orders to combine in such a way that they form a single continuous stream. Any actual decline of demand for the products of a firm is likely in practice to be compounded of two or more of these elements of change, but it is convenient logically to distinguish them, and to analyse their separate effects upon the structure of firms.

§ 2. Permanent Changes of Demand. We have been engaged in earlier chapters in examining the problems of large scale production. It is important to remember a point stressed in an earlier chapter: that large scale production is, in a sense, two-dimensional. We have to consider first the number of units of output which will be produced in a given period of time, and secondly the length of time over which that flow of output will be continued. If a manufacturer is considering

whether or not it will pay him to install some expensive new
plant, he will take both these elements into account.   A very
large flow of output lasting a very short time will offer less
inducement to invest in specialised machinery than a smaller
but more continuous flow.   The production of some trinket or
gadget which satisfies the evanescent whim of the moment is
likely to be met by the adaptation of existing resources rather
than the development of highly specialised plant; but a small
demand, if it be continuous, will justify the purchase of the
most suitable equipment.   The methods of production which
can be profitably employed will depend, therefore, largely
upon the versatility of the machinery available.   The highly
specialised machine is far less common than would appear
from the writings of many economists.   The equipment of
most factories is made up of a quite limited number of
varieties of standard machines, each adapted by comparatively
inexpensive fittings to the particular task it has to perform.

Where this is the case, the manufacturer, when he con-
siders the purchase of a new machine, has to take account
not only of the present flow and probable duration of the
demand for the product which he is at the moment proposing
to manufacture, but also of other commodities which, if the
present demand disappears, he may alternatively produce.
Thus a manufacturer of small plastic components might regard himself as justified in putting in machinery to manufacture such products in general if he could be fairly certain that
components of roughly similar size and character would continue to be demanded, though the exact shape and design
would certainly vary from year to year.   A motor manufacturer will be more ready to install complicated and expensive machinery which possesses sufficient versatility to be
adapted to a new model, when he has to change his design,
than he will be to purchase a machine which is limited to the
output of parts for the existing model.   But the most efficient
machinery is in some industries, and for some purposes in
those industries, very highly specialised.   The cost of tooling-
up a factory to produce a new car may run into many millions

of pounds. It is no accident that the cheapest and most efficiently produced cars are those of which the design has remained almost unaltered over a period of many years.

Where an industry is subject to considerable changes of demand, due either to permanent changes of taste on the part of consumers, or to changes of the methods of production caused by improvements in the thing produced, or in the technique of producing it, that firm will be strongest which can best face the problems of reorganisation and adaptation. The more elaborate a firm is, the more highly specialised in equipment, the better adapted in lay-out to the existing rhythm of production, the more expensive and difficult will be its re-equipment, the more complicated the task of moving and adjusting to their new functions heavy and capricious pieces of machinery. The small firm, by reason of its size, possesses here an advantage. In a large firm, the physical distances involved between departments, and the distances of the location of one process from another, impose heavy punishment on ill-adapted lay-out. The costs and confusion of internal transport will render reorganisation imperative. The smaller firm may be never so well adapted, but will be never so ill adapted, and will enjoy, therefore, a certain advantage where changes of product are frequently necessary, and reorganisation is expensive.

In certain industries and for certain commodities, it seems that there is a cycle of taste and sales. It takes some years for the new product to build up a reputation; when that is built, it enjoys a few years of popularity and large demand, but that again gives way to declining demand as public taste changes, and substitutes of later design take its place. In some trades, the cycle may be as long as ten or fifteen years, in others it is as short as two or three years. In these fashion industries—and fashion rules with electric fittings or carpet sweepers no less powerfully, if with fewer revolutions, than with hats—a firm can seldom be so certain of capturing and retaining the public taste that it can afford to depend wholly on a single article. The wise firm attempts to find a new article while the old one is at the height of its popularity, and to have another commodity just reaching the summit as the old one declines. Within the limits of the versatility of the firm's machinery, the new commodity may be something wholly different, filling a quite distinct want, and selling perhaps in a different market. While the second commodity holds the fort, attempts may be made to recapture the market for the first commodity. For it seems to be the law of succession of design-goods that the crown shall not pass straight. The throne passed from the model T Ford to the later models, not by instantaneous decease and succession, but after a period of intense competition, and Fords have never wholly regained the leadership which they once possessed.

Where the commodities concerned are not such that the optimum technical unit of production is very large, and in particular where the optimum technical unit of production is smaller than the optimum managerial or sales unit, firms producing goods liable to suffer changes of popularity are likely to combine the manufacture of such different commodities as can be made conveniently with the same equipment, and by doing so may succeed in reducing somewhat the risks of considerable fluctuations of demand.

§ 3. **Cyclical Variations of Demand.** So far we have been considering permanent changes in demand, and the power of a firm readily to adapt itself to a different type of production when the demand for the commodity previously produced has disappeared without possibility of recovery. We must next consider the alternative case, where the demand has fallen temporarily, but not, so far as can be judged, permanently. The causes of the trade cycle lie outside the scope of this book; we are concerned here only with the existence of the phenomenon, and its reactions upon the organisation of industry. Before 1914, industry in this and other countries proceeded in a series of spurts and stops. In 1889, in 1899, again in 1906 almost every industry was booming. In 1886, in 1893, and in 1904 almost every industry was depressed.

After the First World War a similar series of booms and depressions recurred, with peaks in 1920, in 1929 and in 1937; in 1921 and in 1931 again almost every industry was depressed. Perhaps with more knowledge and more intelligence, we may learn to control it; since 1945 there has been no depression of similar depth, though there have been several minor set-backs. The existence of such fluctuations continues none-the-less to exercise an influence upon the organisation of industry.

§ 4. A Digression on Short Period Price. If we are to understand how firms are affected by the existence of the cycle and its attendant risks, we must first understand what will be its effects upon price. When a trade depression occurs, it takes the form of a more or less simultaneous, but by no means equal, decline in the demand for almost all goods. Those goods which we have to buy and consume continuously, food, tobacco, newspapers, railway travelling, show the least decline. Those goods whose purchase we can temporarily at least defer, clothes, furniture and boots, show a greater decline. Those goods which are required to increase the production of other goods, machinery, factories, ships, and all the materials that go into them, show the greatest decline. But every producer wants to continue producing; if his works stand idle, the cost is considerable. An idle cotton mill costs some £30,000 a year in standing charges while it produces nothing. Any contribution to overhead costs is better than no contribution, and the cotton manufacturer will be willing to accept a price below the full cost of manufacturing if it yields him some surplus above the prime cost of the goods, a surplus, that is, above those expenses of manufacture of the goods concerned which he would not have incurred if he had not manufactured them. His machinery would be there in any case, he would have to pay interest on debentures and loans in any case; he would have to pay his salaried staff, his foremen, his sales staff; but he would not have to buy the raw material, he would not have to continue to employ some of the lower grades of workers, he would not have to suffer the extra wear and tear of machines, if such there be, over and above the wear and tear of standing idle.   Any price which is greater than these prime costs gives some contribution to the overhead costs of running the business, and it is therefore in the interest of the manufacturer in the short period to accept it, provided that he does not think that by accepting it he will influence the level of other bargains, and so damage himself more than he profits.

The competition of manufacturers who are all prepared if necessary to accept a price lower than the full cost of production, provided that it exceeds the prime cost, may, if the market is weak, force down prices to the level at which it is only just worth while for the producer to continue to produce. The situation is likely to be aggravated by the fact that even those firms whose costs of production are such that the current price is less than their prime costs are not likely to give up without a struggle.   They have an organisation which they do not wish to break up, customers whom they do not wish to lose.   They are therefore likely to continue to produce, for so long as their reserves and their borrowing powers last, at a loss even on prime cost.   Now the fall in price, and the loss as compared with the full costs of production, will depend upon the percentage of total cost which is represented by prime cost.   In a comparatively un-mechanised industry, prime cost will be a fairly high proportion of total cost.   In more mechanised industries, where the capital equipment is elaborate and expensive, the prime cost is a much smaller proportion.

§ 5. **The Readjustment of Industry.**   It can be seen that the more industry advances, the more complex it becomes, the greater is likely to be the upset to prices due to depression of trade.   Now this upset to prices will continue when there is competition so long as the productive capacity of the industry exceeds the demand for the products of the industry at that price at which, at the moment, an efficient firm in the industry can produce and cover its costs.   A new equilibrium between capacity and demand may come about through a general recovery of trade. But if the maladjustment is for any reason greater than can be remedied in that way, the capacity of the industry can be adjusted to the demand only in one of three ways. Firstly, the capacity of the industry may, after a time, diminish. This is a very slow process. Colliery winding engines, looms, ships, locomotives, are still working to-day which were built when our grandfathers were children. At the Soho works, the firm of Avery still employs on occasion the same machines with which Watt built his earliest steam engines. A firm may go bankrupt through the financial strain of a depression, but its equipment is sold to another producer, and the total equipment of the industry is unchanged. Forty years of depression and bankruptcy in the cotton industry have diminished the equipment by little more than that part which has been sold to our foreign competitors. Quick recovery, then, through the reduction of the equipment of the industry is unlikely. The second way in which adjustment may be made is by the demand itself growing, as the result of increasing population and increasing wealth. This is the way in which adjustment was as a rule made during the nineteenth century; but if population ceases to grow this source of recovery will increasingly depend upon the effects of greater income per head. For some products there is a high income-elasticity of demand, but for others the increase of demand with increasing income is small and the help from this source is correspondingly less. Finally, adjustment may be made by such a reduction of the costs of production that, without the existing demand schedule being greatly altered, consumption increases sufficiently to take the whole production of the existing plant off the market; this is the method of efficiency.

Each of these methods is slow and ponderous in operation. Equipment may take twenty or thirty years to wear out. Population grew at its fastest only some 18 per cent in a decade, and that source of adjustment is now fast disappearing. Even reorganisation cannot be achieved in a moment. Meanwhile, firms are making heavy losses. The firms which are strongest may be able to survive such losses for a time, but the time can only be brief. For in most industries the total capital employed by a firm is small as compared with its annual turnover. In the coal industry, the capital of a pit is equal to about one year's turnover. In a steel works, the capital is only about two and a quarter times the value of the annual output. In many other industries the capital/output ratio is below one. The liquid reserves are seldom more than a small proportion of the firm's actual capital. Very few firms have reserves which would enable them to survive a period of depression and readjustment without bankruptcy if the forces of competition were not mitigated and softened by other non-competitive forces. And the more mechanised industry becomes, the greater is likely to become the gap between the average prime cost of a typical firm and the average total cost, so that if prices were driven down to anywhere near prime cost the consequent losses would drain away more rapidly the reserves built up in good years, and financial embarrassment would more quickly overtake even the most efficient.

§ 6. The Effects of Curtailment of Output on Efficiency and Survival. When, because of a depression of trade, the total output of the industry is diminished, the reduction may be brought about in either of two ways. Firstly, the most efficient firms may succeed in under-selling the less efficient, so that the whole reduction of output comes from the elimination of the weakest producers, the most efficient continuing to produce at full capacity. In a world of perfect competition, where no friction existed through the imperfections of markets and the preference of customers for the products of certain firms, and where industry was so localised that transport costs were the same for all firms to all markets, this is the method of curtailment of output that we should expect. But in the world as we know it, with its many and various frictions, reduction of output is usually brought about in the second way, that of reduction by all or almost all the firms in the industry.

It will not be an equal proportionate reduction for all firms, but it will affect them all. Now the large modern firm of to-day is, as we have seen, a most complex organism. Its parts are in a nice balance. It obtains its efficiency through a most difficult co-ordination of its different departments. If we consider a steel firm, for example, the rolling mill, the soaking pits or reheating furnaces, the steel furnaces, the coking plant, the blast furnaces, have been designed in such a way that their output balances when working at full capacity. At that capacity, the plant will be highly efficient. But if for some reason it becomes necessary to produce at 30 per cent less than full capacity, the whole plant will tend to be at sixes and sevens. The most efficient method of producing a small quantity of steel is to produce it in a small furnace, and not in an underworked and over-staffed larger furnace. The plant which is designed for a larger output requires, as a rule, its full team of workers to make it work at all; but that team will be larger than it would have been had it been designed for the reduced output. Moreover, in a steel works which is operating below capacity and by fits and starts, some at least of the designed economies of heat are lost. For they depend upon regular operation and a constant flow. For these reasons, a plant which is more efficient than others at full capacity may yet have a higher cost than the others at an output below its full capacity. From this, two important conclusions follow.

First, the firm which would be the optimum firm in conditions of constant output may not be the optimum firm in conditions of fluctuating output, for it is likely to be too large and too rigid to possess the necessary adjustability. Thus the Balfour Committee reported that 'many blast furnaces are below the standard required for efficient working, and there are few British furnaces equal in size to the large furnaces abroad. It may be remarked, however, that the capacity of the furnaces is to some extent governed by the nature of the product required, and the average volume of orders available throughout the year—circumstances which vary in different countries.'

Second, and very important, the firm which is likely to be selected for us by the natural selection of competition during a depression is not necessarily the most efficient firm if by that we mean the firm which would have the lowest average costs if operating continuously at full capacity. Much play has been made by some writers with the salutary effects of competition and the selective process of the trade depression. This view is based upon a moral interpretation of the doctrine of the survival of the fittest that the biologists would be the first to deny. If there is a famine, and the fodder of the Indian jungle pastures runs short, the cattle begin to die. The first to die are the cows with the calves at foot, the next the heavy milkers; the survivors are the sterile cows, the yielders of little milk. Because these latter have small drain upon them, they can subsist where others die. And so the system of selection in India selects the cow which gives little milk and has no off-spring, and she is doubtless the cow best fitted to survive a famine unaided; but to suggest that she is therefore the most desirable cow from the point of view of the Indian villager would be quite fallacious. The process of the survival of the fittest does not imply that the best survive. It implies only that those survive who do survive; because they survive, we suppose them to have been the fittest to survive.

Now the problem of industrial survival is not quite on a level with this. For a cow cannot in bad times live on the savings of years of plenty, whereas an industrial undertaking can. It might be argued that the firm that we require is neither the firm that is most efficient at full capacity nor that which is most efficient at half capacity, but the firm which over a complete cycle has the lowest average cost of production, taking good times and bad. Even if its costs during bad times are slightly higher than those of its competitors, its profits when working to capacity in good times will be greater, and the reserves that it can build up in good times will enable it to survive the bad times. But in saying this, we have completely shifted our ground. We are no longer saying that the firm which could be in the future the most efficient will survive; we are saying that the firm whose length of life, and whose policy in declaring dividends in the past, has been best adapted to the circumstances will survive. Moreover, the firm which is likely to have the most modern equipment, the firm which was brought into existence during the peak of the preceding boom, will have had no time to build up the necessary financial reserves, and will very probably be one of the first, and not the last, to become insolvent.

This process of selection is still further complicated by the action of the banks. An industrial crisis is in many ways like a shipwreck. In a shipping disaster, we do not speak of the survival of the fittest, for we know that it is not the strongest swimmers, but the weakest that find places in the boats. In an industrial crisis, it is the first firms that become involved that can secure the readiest assistance of the banks. As the banks' funds become tied up, the later applicants, who are in fact the stronger, find assistance more difficult to obtain. Once a firm has secured a seat in the banks' lifeboat, the banks frequently hesitate to throw it overboard in order to find room for another. The indebtedness of a firm to a bank measures the bank's interest in its survival.

For these reasons, we may, I think, conclude that unaided competition does not necessarily select for us the type of firm which in our own interests, as consumers, we would most wish to see remain alive if we were concerned with minimum cost in conditions of full employment. The more strongly we believe that we are going to obtain further control over fluctuations of trade, so that the course of industry will in the future suffer fewer ups and downs, the more we shall hesitate to allow those firms which possess the most modern equipment to be destroyed because of temporary financial embarrassment, when a slight growth of wealth, a slight growth of population, will make them once again valuable possessions. It is of course true, as was said earlier, that bankruptcy does not destroy equipment. The more efficient equipment will survive and probably find purchasers so that it may continue to serve us.　But at the moment, we are concerned not only with the question whether the best equipment will ultimately survive, but also with the question whether the most efficient already existing and operating organisation will survive.　It is to the latter question that we have in many cases to return a negative answer.

§ 7. **Seasonal Variations of Demand.**　We must next proceed to consider the effects upon the structure of firms caused by seasonal changes of demand.　The simplest and most widely adopted method of equalising the flow of production where the demand is seasonal is to manufacture goods at or about the mean rate of consumption, accumulating stocks at seasons of low consumption, reducing stocks at seasons of high consumption.　This method is possible, of course, only where goods can be stored, first without deterioration, second without such addition to cost that it outweighs the economies of more steady production.　Moreover, where fashions or designs are subject to rapid change, or where changes of wage levels and costs are likely, the method of storing may involve such risks that the economy expected is a barely sufficient insurance.　Its profitable adoption will depend in every case upon the rate of interest which must be paid during the period between the time of higher production than consumption, and the time of lower production than consumption.

Where the demand is seasonal and the commodity concerned not storable, two methods of diminishing the fluctuations of production are available.　Firstly, the seasonal commodity may be produced in combination with another commodity which is also seasonal, but whose periods of maximum and minimum activity correspond with the minimum and maximum periods of the commodity first produced.　Thus in the clothing trades summer and winter clothing are often produced together, and the periods of production dovetailed into each other.　Secondly, the seasonal commodity may be produced in combination with another commodity which is not in itself seasonal, but which is, for purposes of providing continuous activity, rendered seasonal. Thus watchmaking or wood-carving has sometimes been made a seasonal winter activity in Switzerland to provide employment for those who in the summer are occupied in agriculture.

The success of this method depends on the conditions in which it is operated. Continuity may be desired either as a method of running versatile equipment continuously, as in the clothing trades, or as a method of keeping together, and keeping employed, skilled labour which would otherwise be dispersed. Where the equipment is versatile, so that overhead costs in each of the trades concerned are reduced, or at least not increased, as compared with a state of affairs in which the trades were conducted separately, this method is likely to be successful. But where the purpose is to keep together a labour force, and where the machinery is not versatile, so that higher overhead costs are incurred in the non-fluctuating trade than would be incurred were it not caused to fluctuate, the method is likely to be unsuccessful unless the gain through keeping workers together is very great. Where there is no great risk of dispersal of the labour force, either because the State provides unemployment benefit, or because the workers, though without alternative source of income, can find no employment, the gain of combining the trades as measured by the narrowest test of profit may be insufficient or negative, but the gain when account is taken of wider considerations, either of State expenditure or of human satisfactions, may be sufficient to justify either an altruistic employer in incurring some slight reduction of profit, or the State in subsidising the provision of equipment in the trade which has been made to fluctuate.

In practice, most of the schemes which have been proposed to reduce the incidence of unemployment among agricultural workers in the winter in temperate climates, in the hot weather in India and other similarly situated countries, have failed for the reason that has been mentioned. The agricultural workers have found themselves in competition with factory workers who can employ machinery twelve months in the year. If similar machinery is to be installed for their use, since it must stand idle half the year, they must accept a wage sufficiently lower than the normal factory wage to compensate for the additional overhead cost. The reduction necessary may be so great that the wage which it would be profitable to offer them would not be worth their while to earn. If on the other hand they attempt to work with old-fashioned hand implements, their output will be so small that the price set by the machine-made goods is again not worth the labour of earning.

§ **8. Erratic Variations of Demand.** We have to consider finally those fluctuations of demand which are irregular, and not periodic. Such fluctuations are likely to occur in those industries in which goods are made not to standardised patterns for sale at a standard price, but to individual orders and designs. Such commodities as shop signs, or specially designed silver-ware, cannot be manufactured in advance and kept in store for prospective customers. But manufacturers of these commodities obtain their custom largely by being able to give the quickest possible delivery. They cannot, therefore, wholly rely on the simplest of all methods of equalising employment, the lengthening and shortening of order books. The even distribution of irregular orders through time will lose them many customers. Moreover, their products, being non-standardised, derive their excellence from the skilled craftsmanship of the workers that have been brought together, and it is particularly important to avoid their dispersal.

It is common, therefore, to combine the manufacture of some irregularly produced speciality with the manufacture of some standardised secondary product, often requiring far less skill on the part of the worker. The main profit of the firm is made out of the speciality. The secondary product serves only as a means of keeping together the skilled workers in times of shortage of orders, and may barely cover the prime

costs of its own operation.   There are, in the Birmingham and
Sheffield districts, certain products which are standard secondary products of firms whose main preoccupation is with a
speciality which enjoys a profitable but uncertain market;
these secondary products are often produced, and sold at
prices which to a firm specialised in their production would
be unprofitable.   In some cases, the secondary product is
produced intermittently by those workers who are for the
moment not engaged on the primary product; in other cases,
the secondary product is produced continuously, at some times
by the skilled workers who are momentarily free, at others by
less skilled workers—on occasion by married women formerly
in the firms' employment—who are engaged and discharged
as required.

§ 9. Combination and Risk.   Our argument thus far has led
us to the conclusion that the existence of risks and fluctuations
leads in general to smaller but more flexible units, and in
particular to smaller technical units, than would be economical were production carried on continuously and evenly.   This
influence, in conjunction with the constant pressure of the
limitations of the local market, drives producers in narrower
and more fluctuating markets to perfect the technical development of the small plant.   While richer countries, and in
particular the United States, have brought the economy of the
large plant to a high level of achievement, the poorer countries, with whom for these purposes we must group ourselves,
have attempted rather to secure the efficient organisation of
the small unit.   There is, however, something more to be said.
The effects both of cyclical and permanent declines in demand
may be less damaging to individual producers if they can agree
to act in concert, and in certain cases, the existence of risks
may lead, therefore, not to smaller, but to considerably larger
units of production.

To understand what steps a manufacturer or group of
manufacturers must take in order to diminish the risks of a
general decline of demand, we must consider for a moment

how the ordinary competitive economic system operates when
left to itself. It works through a system of rewards and
punishments. We know that when there is a shortage, prices
rise; when there is a glut, prices fall. This means that when
the manufacturer provides too little, he is rewarded for his
stinginess; when he provides too much, he is fined for his
generosity; which, if one thinks about it dispassionately, is
an extremely paradoxical way of ordering an economic system. A visitor from the other side of the looking glass might
well have expected us to arrange things so that when a boot
manufacturer out of the goodness of his heart makes so many
boots that everyone may have enough, he would be rewarded;
when he fails to supply us with enough boots, he would be
punished; but that is not the way we do things.

If a manufacturer is to be fined every time that he produces
too much, it is natural that he should take great trouble to
see that he does not turn out so much that he will get punished.
But we must remember that the price depends not, as a rule,
on the amount turned out by any one manufacturer but on
the amount turned out by all the makers of the commodity
together. Where there is perfect competition, and no open
or tacit understanding, each manufacturer turns out as much
as he profitably can; for each manufacturer wants to increase
his share of the total, while he hopes that because of a contraction of output by other manufacturers, the total will be as
small as possible, and that he will get a high price for all his
goods. When there are a great many independent producers,
as there are in agriculture, and as there have been till lately
in coal mining, this system of rewards and punishments works
in an effective, if somewhat heavy-handed, way. But when
there are comparatively few producers, they begin to look
round for methods of escaping the fines and enjoying the
rewards all the time.

Now supposing all the manufacturers can agree simultaneously to limit their individual outputs, the price which
can be charged will be higher, and the profit on each unit
of output greater. It will very likely be to the interest of the

individual producer to limit his output provided that others do the same. For the individual producer wants to make the greatest total profit. He can either have a large profit on each of a small number of units of output or a small profit on each of a large number of units of output. There will be for him one output which will give him the greatest total profit, that is when the profit per unit, multiplied by the number of units that he can sell, is greatest. Our individual producer would like to have a large output with a large margin of profit; but the margin of profit is only large when the total output is small, and it may be very unlikely that other producers will diminish their production. In these circumstances, it will often be to the interest of a manufacturer to accept a smaller share of a very profitable market rather than to aim at securing a larger share of a less profitable market. And so we find concerted arrangements for the limitation of output.

The problem of how far monopolists can diminish fluctuations of demand and fluctuations of profit must be left to the volume of this series which deals with Monopoly. For the moment, we are concerned with the reactions of this type of risk, and of the methods of diminishing the risk, on the size of firms. It is evident that the size of firms has no effect on the risk, except in so far as the firm becomes of such size that the formation of a monopoly is facilitated. Firstly, therefore, there will be an advantage to those firms which in their individual industries become so large that they enjoy a position of monopoly. It may be to the interest of an undertaking to grow to a size greater than that which will secure it the greatest efficiency if by that growth it can secure monopoly gains which outweigh, as they almost certainly will, the losses due to this excessive size. Secondly, the collaboration of separate firms in monopolistic associations is far easier and far more likely to be successful where the firms whose interests must be harmonised are few. Informal agreements can be made and honoured among a dozen firms which cannot be carried through where there are twelve hundred firms. The possibility of monopoly action may then lead to the building up of units larger than would otherwise be established. Moreover, once a monopolistic association of firms has been formed, it may in certain circumstances be to the interest of one particular firm or combination of firms to increase its scale of operations still further, in order that its participation in the association may be greater, and its influence on the policy of the association correspondingly increased. In these two ways, the existence of this type of risk may affect the size of firms, making them in this case larger than they otherwise would have been. But its influence on industrial structure must be limited to these comparatively rare possibilities. Where monopoly is out of question, or association can be achieved as easily with firms of normal size as with larger units, the existence of the risk of a general maladjustment of capacity to output will be no inducement to the formation either of larger or smaller units, except so far as those considerations of technical economy or of the risks of total loss of market prevail which were discussed on an earlier page.

§ **10. Technical Progress and Risk.** There is one important respect in which size may diminish risk. In general the risk of being faced with a long-term diminution of demand such as was discussed at the beginning of this chapter is greatest for the firm whose products are becoming obsolete and least for the firm which is in the vanguard of technical progress. The technically backward firm is always tending to lose customers, the technically advanced firm is always tending to attract them.

How far is size associated with technical advance? It is difficult to give a categorical answer. It has already been argued that the small firm is often in a position to adjust its production more quickly to the changing needs of the market. In many industries the most attractive products come from relatively small firms. There is, however, one powerful factor on the other side. In an increasing number of industries technical progress depends to a greater and greater extent upon scientific research. If one studies the distribution of scientific research in industry one finds a very large proportion of it concentrated in the big firms, and particularly in the 250 or so biggest firms.

The reasons for this are self-evident. The small firm, with 250 or fewer employees, can only exceptionally afford to do any serious research at all; there are of course a few exceptions where a small specialist firm in a narrow market lives by exploiting some new and developing technique. The medium-sized firm, though it may engage in research, can at best hardly support a really viable research team. The powerful research team, with first-class workers capable of cracking the difficult problems, is mainly to be found in the really big firm.

This does not mean that the smaller firms are wholly cut off from research. In many industries, and in particular in the industries predominantly organised in small firms, cooperative research is organised in Research Associations with the assistance and financial support of the Department of Scientific and Industrial Research. Where the need is for the solution of the general scientific problems of an industry or for minor scientific trouble-shooting, this co-operative research is invaluable. But inevitably it does not give individual firms help at all comparable with that which the research departments of some of the biggest firms provide by way of developing new products or new methods exclusively available to the firm concerned.

§ 11. Spreading Risks. In this chapter we have seen that the existence of risks may modify in various ways the size and form of organisation of the optimum firm. It remains to discuss one principal way in which this may operate. In a world in which there was no uncertainty and no change we might expect very large and very specialised plants, enjoying all the economies of running perpetually at full capacity. We have already seen in an earlier chapter how the introduction of the more dynamic problems of change, risk and uncertainty may affect the size of the firm that can be effectively managed.

Equally it will affect the choice of products. We have seen in this chapter that the pattern of commodities being produced is constantly changing in detail. What a firm produces to-day is nearly always different from what the firm produced ten years ago. To-day the firm is trying to guess what its possible customers will want to buy from it ten years hence and to make its preparations accordingly.

In making its decisions the firm may, if it is brave, back its judgment that if it concentrates all its resources on making some new product, or some old product greatly improved, it can keep its capital profitably employed and its employees fully at work. But in many cases a firm, either from cowardice or prudence, will prefer to spread its risks. It will introduce new products while going ahead with old products. It will try tentatively to see whether it can make a success of some new line of business while clinging also to the things in which it knows that it has experience. Thus out of uncertainty grows the multi-product firm, dividing its energies and resources between a variety of types of output.

The problems of the multi-product firm will be discussed more fully in a later chapter. It is not easy to say how far the multi-product firm is, by the very fact of spreading its activities, less efficient. Some spreading of risks and some attempt to use more than one market to keep non-specific equipment fully employed is often a wise policy. But there is reason to think that British industry pushes this policy too far, so as to lose some of the advantages gained by many American firms in concentrating their energies upon a narrower range of products. It would seem very doubtful whether all British firms have really assessed realistically the cost of undertaking small batches of extraneous production, often interrupting a flow of work and involving twice-over, before and after, a re-setting of equipment. A ruthless pruning of non-economic production is one of the essentials of profitable risk-spreading.

CHAPTER VII

THE RECONCILIATION OF DIFFERING OPTIMA

§ 1. The Problem of Reconciliation. We have seen in the preceding chapters that for certain technical purposes large scale production is necessary, or at the least advantageous, that for certain other purposes such large scale is neither necessary nor desirable. We have seen that in certain respects a very large business can be managed more effectively than a small one, or so organised by its management that its productive processes are more efficiently carried on. In other cases, however, a large firm is at a disadvantage in this respect; a small firm can achieve as successful or even more successful results. Even where the management of a large firm can show a balance of advantage over that of a smaller, this is likely to be due to the fact that from certain functions of management gains are still to be secured, though from certain other functions losses are already arising. It may happen, again, that the scale of the manufacturing departments has reached and passed its optimum size, but economies are still to be secured from buying material on a larger scale or from selling on a larger scale, for there is no reason to suppose that all the different functions of management and of manufacture will reach their optimum size at one and the same total output of the product. The problem, therefore, arises of reconciling the different optimum sizes of different parts of the same organisation. As was suggested in the second chapter, this reconciliation may be brought about by attempting to make different parts of the organisation work efficiently at the same size. Where, as is sometimes the case, the technical optimum size is in danger of becoming greater than the managerial optimum, efforts may be made to increase the efficiency of management, to make it more human, and in closer touch with the workers by various devices. Much thought in recent years has been devoted to this problem of increasing the efficiency and the smooth co-ordination of large productive units, but it cannot be said that the problem has been solved. Success, where it has been achieved, has been due usually to the personality and influence of a single man.

The more usual method of approach to this problem is the attempt, by various devices of industrial organisation, to put each different function of production and management on its own optimum scale, and to bring them together by a common control where the form adopted requires this. The way in which this may be done can be best explained by a few examples. Maladjustment of the optima of different functions will arise sometimes from a technical optimum larger than can be effectively managed with the managerial talent available, sometimes from a technical optimum too small for effective management, sometimes from a scale of optimum financial control larger than the technical optimum (it is seldom in fact smaller), sometimes again from an optimum scale of marketing larger than the optimum scale of production.

Let us start by considering the problem of the technical optimum which is larger than the managerial optimum with available managerial talent. The solution which is usually adopted here is the breaking up of the firm into various wholly separate departments. This is a fairly common practice, for example, in the motor industry. The Morris Division of the British Motors Corporation builds its engines at Coventry and Birmingham, its commercial vehicles at Birmingham, its radiators in Oxford, its bodies in a separate organisation at Cowley, and the whole are finally assembled in the big shops at Cowley. Ford employed for a time at least a somewhat similar division of his total organisation. He located different small plants, manufacturing such parts as headlights, wheels, generator cut-outs, in small villages and towns on the banks of the Rouge River and the Huron River, employing the local labour supply to operate it. Their work was co-ordinated and planned by the central management. The local managerial staff was usually of very small dimensions, since one or two men sufficed in most cases to manage the plant and keep the records.

It is, of course, difficult to be certain in all these cases that this division is due to economic and not to historic reasons. In very many cases, moreover, where this method has in fact been adopted, it is not obvious to the external observer, who is likely to notice it only where departments are separated geographically as well as in organisation. In many large firms the division between departments is a very rigid boundary, and the departments are co-ordinated only by the financial and planning control of the higher administration. In this way the unit of actual organisation is kept sufficiently small to be manageable by persons of the ability that is available. In many industries, however, such division into departments is for technical reasons impossible. In such cases a rather different method of dealing with the problem of the larger technical than managerial unit is to be found. An attempt is made to reduce the optimum size of the technical unit by increasing its specialisation.

§ 2. Vertical Disintegration. There is another solution frequently to be discovered of the problem that arises when the optimum technical unit is larger than the optimum managerial unit. Some reference to it was made in the second chapter, where I called it the method of Vertical Disintegration. Where the technical unit requires to be large, not because all the processes require to be on a large scale, but because one process requires to be on a large scale, that process tends to be separated off and performed for the main industry by another subsidiary industry. Thus motor firms buy such parts as the electrical equipment from outside. Bevel gears for back-axles are manufactured for themselves only by the largest firms and by the smallest. The doctrine of self-sufficiency in this respect is followed on grounds of economy by the very large firm; it is followed also, in most cases rather for reasons of quality than of cheapness, by the very much smaller producer who aims at the highest technical perfection. Even the Ford works, which long prided itself on its self-sufficiency, adopted in the 1930s the policy of buying many parts from outside specialist firms. By such outside purchase the small firm can obtain almost all the economies available to the large firm. It is at a disadvantage only in so far as its smaller demands enable it to drive a less hard bargain with the specialist firm. A similar distinction between the optimum sizes of different processes of production is found in the cotton industry. The technical optimum here is comparatively small for spinning and weaving. For finishing it is very much larger. It has consequently been the practice from the time of the industrial revolution for spinning and weaving to be carried on separately from finishing; and the finishing firms have always been fewer than the weaving firms.

This continuous separation of processes into industries has been in the past a very important source of saving and of increased output. It is interesting to contrast, as Professor Allyn Young has done, the industries of varying scale which now contribute to the making of a book with the far less divided and specialised labours of the mediæval scribe. By the separation of the other processes from publishing, the small publisher became possible. A publisher's business to-day need not be on that scale which will secure the greatest possible economy of ink-making, of printing machinery manufacture, of paper manufacture, of colour reproduction, or even of printing. All, or any, of these tasks can be assigned to the large specialist firms which work for the whole industry. Many of the leading publishers possess no printing works of their own. The provision of bread similarly includes processes on all scales of production. The small individual farmer, the large importer, the very large miller, the small distributor, the tiny local bakery, are all able to operate on their own best scale.

The device of vertical disintegration is the commonest method of dealing with a single process which requires a scale larger than is required by other processes.   But it may sometimes happen that the optimum managerial or financial unit corresponds not to the remaining small scale processes, but to the larger scale of that process which under vertical disintegration would be separated from the others.   In this case two alternative forms of reconciliation exist.   The adoption of one rather than the other will depend upon the versatility of the equipment required for the individual large scale process. By the first method, the scale of the technical production of a single commodity is increased, without as a rule incurring any diseconomies, to correspond with the scale of management and of the individual large scale process.   By the second method, two or more commodities are manufactured together in order that they may together keep fully occupied the large scale process, which must in this case be adaptable to alternative final commodities at little cost.

Thus it may be necessary, in order to secure the greatest economies, that certain basic processes shall be on a large scale. The remaining processes may reach their optimum scale, with the greatest division of labour and the greatest integration of processes, while demanding a smaller output from the preparatory processes than will establish them upon an optimum scale. It might happen, for instance, that in a works manufacturing light brass goods, a department making taps and a department making furniture fittings could each secure the greatest available efficiency while comparatively small, whereas the foundry was still obtaining economies as the total output of brass goods of all sorts by the firm was increasing.   In this case, it may be a matter of complete indifference whether the firm grows by increasing its production of taps only, multiplying in parallel the processes for producing taps, but securing no further economies in the production of taps, or whether it grows by adding a furniture fittings department.   Either plan will have the effect of increasing the scale of production in the foundry, the department in which an increase in scale is desirable. Either plan will increase its efficiency, if, as is probable, that is dependent not on a high degree of standardisation in the department, but rather on a large output of castings of all types.

§ 3. **Further Devices for Reconciliation.** Let us now consider the opposite case, where the managerial optimum is larger than the technical optimum. In this case, the simplest solution is the ordinary very large firm; the optimum technical scale is simply reproduced several times over. No further division of labour, and no further integration of processes, is secured by such multiplication. On the other hand, except for possible diseconomies of internal transport within the factory, there are no losses to be suffered by such growth. Such diseconomies as are encountered are outweighed by the gains of the larger and more efficient management.

But here again, as in the last case, a choice of methods is open. If the advantages of large scale management arise from the employment of specialists who are expert in some broad functions, labour management for instance, which are hardly concerned with the nature of the final product, or expert with regard to a group of similar products rather than one specialised product, brass turning and finishing for instance, there may be little or no economy to be obtained by multiplying identical technical units rather than broadly similar technical units. To take the same example as was taken in a preceding paragraph, if the optimum technical scale of the manufacture of taps is small, and the optimum technical scale for the manufacture of furniture fittings is small, it may be possible to enjoy the advantages of large scale management, either by having a large firm manufacturing only taps, or by having a large firm manufacturing only furniture fittings, or by having a large firm manufacturing both taps and furniture fittings. It would in this case be erroneous to suppose that the existence of several firms not wholly specialised as regards the final product was evidence of a wasteful or uneconomic system of production. More must be said of this when we come to consider the added complications of marketing.

We have still to examine another type of solution to this problem of reconciling the small technical unit and the large management unit. In the two cases which we have so far considered, the management and the multiplied technical units have all been assumed to be in the same place. Now, in certain cases where the technical unit is small, an advantage may be secured by placing the small technical units not together, but in different places; in this way, transport costs may be reduced to a minimum. The United States Steel Corporation, for instance, operates under a single managing control many plants distributed all over the United States. By this system of distribution, long freights may be avoided. Orders are distributed to individual plants by the central management; wherever a high degree of specialisation does not give very considerable economies, such distribution of plant may be advantageous even though the optimum technical unit is not reached, for the advantage of specialisation is more than offset by the extra costs of transport involved. This is the more likely to happen where customs barriers intervene. Thus Ford distributes the assembly of his cars not only for foreign markets but also for the United States market in different centres in such a way that, taking local costs of production and transport and tariffs into consideration, he obtains the greatest possible economy, even though individual plants may fall below the efficiency of the Detroit plant. The large brewery companies similarly maintain a number of breweries so distributed that they can best supply a widely spread market.

It may happen that the small technical unit and the larger managerial unit will require to be combined for another reason. We have seen that for the purposes of a fluctuating output, due either to seasonal or cyclical demands, a small technical unit is likely to be more adaptable and economical than the largest possible technical unit. Where this is the case, the best organisation of a firm may be a multiplicity of

small technical units working under a single large management. These small technical units may be concentrated at a
single point, or located at different points in the market to be
served, according as the saving of cross freights or the saving
of management costs is greater. But in this connection, one
further point must be observed. The large firm combining
several technical units under a single management can concentrate production in times of low output into one or more
of these several technical units, and allow the remaining units
to stand completely idle, or to produce only the difference
between what the firm sells and what its best plant or plants
can produce. Where this is possible, and the total output of
the firm considerably exceeds that of one optimum technical
unit, the structure of the firm is likely to take the form of one
or more plants which can secure the greatest possible economy
if run continuously to full capacity, and other plants which
possess predominantly the virtue of economical adaptability
to all different scales of output. An example of this type of
organisation is to be found in the case of electricity supply.
Certain selected stations carry the base load. This is to be
the function of the nuclear stations among others. Other
stations meet the daily peak loads. Others again provide for
even further seasonal and occasional peaks of demand. This
type of organisation is possible only to the very large firm
or to an association of firms with close working agreements.
It is open to the objection that it is likely, while reducing
fluctuations of employment in one place, to increase both the
intensity and duration of unemployment in other places.

The problem of reconciling the smaller manufacturing
optimum with the larger sales optimum was examined at some
length in the chapter devoted to the problems of marketing.
It was seen there that the same device of vertical disintegration, which enables small producers to escape from the tyranny
of processes demanding large scale, can be applied also to the
difficulty of large scale marketing. The task is separated off
and entrusted to specialists working on the appropriate scale.
It was seen also that in very many cases an advantage lay

with manufacturers who produce a line of different articles which could be sold together, since the economies on the side of sales were more important than the possible economies to be secured by making one individual article on a larger scale. It is evident that this consideration will influence the choice of the method of expansion in cases such as those which we have been considering, where the technical optimum is smaller than the managerial or financial optimum. The method of expansion by producing two similar articles will be preferred to the method of expansion by producing a single article on a larger scale without any considerable further economies.

Within the structure of selling organisations themselves, the same problem of reconciling divergent optima arises. The ordinary unit of retail selling, the shop, is limited in size by the local market, and seldom, it would appear, reaches its optimum scale. Management, buying, and financial control all require a larger scale for their most efficient employment. In some trades, attempts are made by expensive advertising to attract customers to the larger units. In other trades, the same device is employed which we have already considered as regards small technical units. The local units are controlled by a centralised management. Thus we find in the retail market the chain stores with comparatively little initiative in the hands of the local manager, and the important decisions of policy, of buying, and of finance in the hands of the central organisation. In other cases again a solution is sought by multiplying the range of products sold by the single shop, and we find the familiar departmental store.

A complete description of all the devices which are in practice used for reconciling different optimum units is beyond the scope of this book. Some indication here has been given of the more typical methods employed. In conclusion, a word of warning is necessary. I have found, I think, more reason than is usually found to justify the actions of manufacturers who produce on a small scale, who combine different products in a single factory, or sell them with a single sales staff. Much that I have said depends upon the condition that optimum technical units of production are smaller than optimum sales or management units. With present methods of production, economies may perhaps be discovered in some industries in combining different activities in the way that I have described. But if the optimum technical unit, employing the best equipment which could be designed, were larger, the organisation would need, in all probability, drastic revision. Not all those industries in which the prevailing method is that of small scale production and the manufacture of all and everything under a single roof are to be commended for their economic wisdom.

CHAPTER VIII

THE PROBLEM OF GROWTH

§ 1. The Cost of Growth. We have seen in previous chapters that in certain circumstances the large firm will have an advantage over its smaller rival. We have next to consider how the small firm can increase its scale of operations so as to secure the maximum economies, and how far in ordinary competitive conditions it will be to its interest to secure these economies. The individual firm has to consider not only the gains to be secured by growth, but also the costs of growth, and if in fact the costs of growing exceed the gains of growing, the optimum scale of production may not in certain circumstances be achieved by the ordinary processes of competition. We shall have at a later stage to consider the costs of growth, and how far these costs can be altered by different methods of growth. For the time being, we must consider in what ways competition may tend to establish firms of other than the optimum size.

First of all, we have seen that where a market is not perfect, there is a capital cost of transferring customers from one firm to another. The more imperfect the market, the higher will this capital cost be, and the more of the customers of a firm it is sought to transfer, the higher the cost is likely to be for each additional customer, as we proceed from the less firmly attached customers to the more firmly attached customers. Sooner or later, a point may be reached where the extra cost of attracting customers is not justified by the extra economy to be obtained from operation on a larger scale. But the point where this equilibrium will be reached will depend upon the conditions of the trade. If the advantages of operating near the optimum scale are great, and the costs of transferring customers small, possibly because total demand for the product is increasing rapidly, the firms are likely to reach a size nearer to the optimum size than where these conditions do not prevail. The transfer is likely to be easiest where the customer is a good judge of the quality of the thing he is buying; it is likely to be most expensive where his judgment is warped either by fashion or by advertisement.

Secondly, we have seen that growth to the technically most efficient scale may be delayed or rendered impossible by the accidents of an unusual depression of trade which yields an undue temporary advantage to older firms and to firms with plant which can be operated efficiently below full capacity. The promising new firm is likely to be cut off in infancy since it will not have had the time in which to establish the financial strength which is as necessary a condition of survival as technical strength.

§ 2. The Discontinuity of Increases of Efficiency.

These are obvious impediments to the establishment by competition of the optimum firm. There is another which is in certain conditions even more important. The assumption that competition tends to establish the most efficient scale of production implies the assumption that all scales of production are increasingly more efficient up to the optimum size, and that a firm is therefore led on automatically from stage to stage. But in some industries at least there is very grave reason to doubt this assumption. In the figures of the size of firms in the cotton industry, for example, we can find clear traces of considerable groupings of firms at scales of production other than that of 100,000 spindles. In agriculture, we can find at least two sizes of farm which can be regarded as optima, separated by intervening sizes which seem to be less efficient than either of the two optima. In several industries we can find evidence of what we may, perhaps, call a 'Pessimum Firm.' It is a size of firm which combines the technical disadvantages of smallness with the managerial disadvantages of being too large for individual control. In some industries it would appear that there is a tendency for firms to fail at one particular critical size, a size usually that entails a departure from individual management and a local market, in the direction of organised and co-ordinated management, and a national market. The problem of growth in these industries is the problem of jumping over or rushing through this pessimum size, and the ultimate attainment of the optimum scale of production depends upon the possession of sufficient strength or momentum to carry the small growing firm through the critical point. It is by no means clear that the power to pass the critical point is the best criterion of a firm's subsequent right to survive on a wholly different scale of production. To take an analogy from a very different field, the Supermarine S6 which ultimately won the Schneider Trophy race failed with the propeller first fitted to get through the critical hydroplaning speed of about twenty-five knots. It was only when a propeller allowing a lower maximum speed had been fitted that it could pass this point of hump resistance and get into the air at all. A seaplane with one quarter of its maximum speed would have had no difficulty whatever in passing the critical point. In much the same way, a firm, which is over-optimistically designed for ultimate large scale production, may be less well equipped for the initial stages of its career than a firm which is not designed with a view to future growth.

Now, if there are a number of minor optima in an industry and one larger major optimum, we should expect the normal methods of growth to be different from those which we should find in an industry with a steady progression of economies. Moreover, the methods will be likely to differ according to the circumstances of demand in the industry. For the rate of growth of new firms is likely to be more rapid where demand is growing, and the new firms are adding to an existing output, than where demand is steady and the new firms have to substitute their output for the output of existing firms. The rate of growth of new firms is likely to be slowest and most expensive where demand is declining and old firms are being driven to improve their efficiency in order to maintain their existing outputs. It is therefore in times of good trade and increasing output that new firms are most likely to succeed in establishing themselves, and in rushing on the wave of prosperity and large margins of profit through the pessimum point. Success here will depend upon the width of the gap between the minor and major optima. If it is a wide gap, it may be impossible that it should be rushed in this way. If for example the optima in agriculture are represented by a farm of 50 acres and a farm of 2,000 acres, no boom will suddenly make the little farmer into the big farmer. It involves a complete change of method, of outlook and of experience which could not possibly be acquired in a few months of hectic expansion. On the other hand, Lord Nuffield managed to grow from being a small efficient manufacturer of 3,000 cars a year to what was then a large scale producer of 50,000 cars a year in the period between 1921 and 1925 in the face of a trade depression.

§ 3. Expansion and Combination.

Where the gap between the minor and major optima is a wide one, growth to the major optimum by expansion from the minor optimum will be impossible. In such cases it may be possible to start at a scale of production not considerably smaller than the major optimum, and to expand towards it. Thus a new steel plant would not be started on a small scale with the intention of later expansion, but on a scale close to that of any of the leading plants of the country. To start successfully on the largest scale of production, it is necessary that demand should be readily and cheaply diverted to the new source of supply. It is this reason that probably accounts for the fact that an almost negligible part of the present output of steel is derived from new firms which have started, unconnected with older firms, since the beginning of the twentieth century.

Where there is little possibility of ready and cheap diversion, the most common method of growth is the combination of a number of firms, possibly, but by no means certainly, all of the scale of the minor optimum, into one firm or organisation on the scale of the major optimum. By this combination, the need for diversion of demand is avoided. The constituent firms of the combination bring to it their small individual attached markets, and the scale of operation of the combination can from the first be that of an optimum firm. Moreover, the cost of growth will be considerably diminished, for neither expensive advertisement nor cut-throat competition is necessary to secure the required demand.

Such combination may take as many different shapes as the old man of the sea. We may start, however, by distinguishing two main types of industrial combination which have been called respectively 'vertical combinations' and 'horizontal combinations.' Horizontal combination is the combination of firms in the same stage of production to secure a larger scale of operation of that particular process or group of processes. The recent combinations of many motor omnibus companies, or of cotton spinning companies, to form larger omnibus companies or larger cotton spinning corporations, afford us examples of horizontal combination. It is with horizontal combination that we have been concerned in the preceding paragraphs, and no further examination of it is now required. Vertical combination on the other hand is the combination of firms in successive stages of the same industry. Thus a steel-making firm may secure its supplies of raw material by buying coal mines and iron ore supplies; it may secure a market for its plates by acquiring control of a shipbuilding firm.

The causes which lead to vertical combination are in general wholly different from those which favour horizontal combination. We have seen in an earlier chapter that where, in consequence of a change of technique, one process or group of processes requires to be performed on a larger scale than the other processes of that industry, that particular process will tend to be separated off from the main process, and entrusted to a specialist firm. We called this separation 'vertical disintegration.' If on the other hand some change of technique restores the optimum scale of production of this particular process to equality with that of the main industry, either by increasing the optimum scale of the one or diminishing that of the other, then the reasons for separation will have disappeared, and convenience of single control may lead to a re-establishment of a single undivided series of processes. We may call this reunion of the separated processes 'vertical combination,' or for symmetry, if we prefer it, 'vertical integration.'

The tendency towards vertical integration will be reinforced where particular economies are to be obtained from performing certain processes either in close proximity to each other or in quick series one after the other. In the first case, unnecessary handling and transport may be avoided; in the second, economies either of time or of heat may be obtained. These latter economies are to be discovered in particular in the iron and steel industries. In the early days of the iron and steel trade, the separation of iron manufacture from steelmaking was common. In this century, the technique of production has changed in such a way as to yield considerable fuel economies where coking-ovens, blast furnaces, steel furnaces and rolling mills are all closely united at one spot and under one control. Vertical integration is here the consequence of these economies, and the boundary between industry and industry can be seen to be shifting with alterations of technique and knowledge, at one moment dividing, at another reuniting processes to form the constantly changing groups of processes which for the time being compose an industry. Some industries, weaving, for instance, consist of but one or two processes; others, such as bootmaking, of several hundred. Some subsidiary industries abstract a single process, others again a whole series of complicated processes. There is nothing in the fundamental nature of things which would separate spinning from weaving, and not the making of uppers from the making of soles. A few years and a few inventions may reunite the first and divide the second.

§ **4. Types of Vertical Integration.** Vertical integration is sometimes the consequence of a reuniting of separated processes to obtain economies. It is more often the consequence of a search for security. We may for purposes of clarity separate two main types of vertical integration. We may call them 'forward integration' and 'backward integration.' These terms assume that the dominant partner in the integration can be distinguished, and they seek to analyse the motives of this dominant partner. His motives may be either the securing of markets by forward integration, or of sources of raw material by backward integration. Thus a steel firm may at one moment find it necessary to secure its sources of raw materials by backward integration, if it has reason to think that the prices of those materials are likely to be raised against it by the competition of rival steel producers. But the gain in times of high prices that is secured by the ownership of the sources of raw materials is to some extent offset in periods of low prices by the losses which may be incurred through the compulsory purchase of materials from one given source. Thus, before the nationalisation of coal, managers of steel plants with associated collieries found themselves from time to time at a disadvantage as compared with their rivals in that they were obliged to accept coal at cost price from the associated colliery, while their rivals obtained it below cost price in the open market. Profits are likely, therefore, to be greater in time of prosperity and less in time of depression where raw material supplies are controlled, if transfers from one member of the combination to another are made at cost price. But this greater variation of profit applies only to the dominant partner in the combination, and the fluctuations of profits of the whole combination treated as a unit are likely to be no greater and no smaller under conditions of competition than the sum of those of the constituent parts.

Where one or more of the raw materials are monopolised, there will be a clear advantage to the raw material consuming firm if it can partake in the monopoly and obtain its materials at the cost of production plus the necessary return on the capital invested, rather than at the monopoly price.   The gain will be even greater if for any reason the cost of production of the raw material is less, either through more regular working or through working more nearly at full capacity, to the associated supplier of the raw material than to the unassociated supplier.   Owing to the monopolisation of the production of raw materials in Germany and to the existence of the economies just described where mixed firms own, for example, both coal mines and iron and steel furnaces, vertical integration has proceeded much further than it has hitherto in this country, where raw materials have remained unmonopolised.

Let us now turn to forward integration.   The purpose of this is to secure markets and outlets for the production of the dominant partner in the integration.   We should expect to find this type of integration most frequently where the final product is competing with other products not only on the basis of price, but also on the basis of quality.   For integration with marketing organisations is most advantageous where its purpose is to induce the retailer to recommend the product of the dominant partner in the integration rather than similar products offered by rival producers at about the same price. But it is to be found also where there are considerable economies of production to be obtained by constant and steady operation, or by operation at full capacity rather than at half capacity.   As examples of the first, we find brewers buying public houses and tying them to their own beers, boot manufacturers buying retail shops in order to market their own products in preference to those of their rivals, collieries interested in coal selling agencies, meat shippers controlling retail butchers' shops, film producing companies owning circles of cinemas.   Of the second type, we find steel firms associated with shipbuilding firms as an outlet for their steel, with makers of screws, nuts and bolts, with firms specialising in structural work, and in railway locomotive or waggon manufacture.

There is one primary distinction which we must make between forward and backward integration.   Forward integrations are likely to be formed at moments when productive capacity outruns consumption, for their purpose is the appropriation of certain markets. They are likely therefore to be formed in times of bad trade. They will be weakest, because least necessary, in times of good trade. On the other hand, backward integrations are likely to be formed in times of good trade, since they exist to prevent owners of temporarily limited supplies of raw material exploiting the consuming firms. They will be weakest, perhaps they will even break up, in times of depression.

It would be wrong to suppose that all vertical combinations can be readily divided into forward or backward integration. There are many instances in which apparently equal partners combine for their mutual interest and in which this convenient division would not be applicable. Let us consider briefly the motives that may lead to such combination. It may, as has been suggested already, be the consequence simply of the reunion of previously divided processes where the optimum scale has now become approximately equal. This tendency may be reinforced by other economies. We have seen that where the managerial unit is considerably larger than the technical unit, the two may be reconciled either by a multi-plication of identical technical units under one control, or by the combination of several different technical units under one control. These different technical units may either be para-llel units, manufacturing perhaps different products from the same material, or they may be successive units, performing a series of processes in the production of a single final commodity. If the optimum managerial unit has increased more rapidly than the optimum technical unit, we might expect to find the two reconciled by increased vertical com-bination. This tendency will be supported by considerations of capital raising. For the necessary capital for the exploita-tion of a new source of raw material, which is likely to be highly speculative, can be raised more cheaply by a firm of established reputation which will consume the output, than by a group of comparatively unknown promoters with no security other than that of the enterprise itself.   Moreover, the consuming firm can give to its own sources of supply a known market, deriving from outside sources the remainder of its requirements, and throwing on to them the greater risk.   In certain cases, the development of such resources may require more capital than could be borrowed on reasonable terms by a new enterprise, and better political and financial terms for the development may be secured by an existing firm of reputation and standing.   It was probably such considerations as these which led Unilever to explore the sources of their materials, Dunlop's to embark in rubber growing.

In certain other areas, the possession of means of distributing retail goods has led to the establishment or the control of sources for the supply of those goods, either because existing suppliers were using the reputation of brands to obtain monopoly prices, or because it was desired to secure products of a required purity or quality.   Thus out of the Co-operative Movement has grown the great Co-operative Wholesale Society, providing local Co-operative Stores with certain brands of goods whose monopoly price enhances the profits and dividends of the Co-operative Movement rather than of private producers.   Boot's chemists shops retail many branded goods manufactured by the wholesale department of the same firm; Lipton's own tea plantations.   In all these instances, the safe and known market for their products reduces the risks of the producing side of the business as compared with those of unintegrated producers.

Great Britain has hitherto seen less vertical integration than almost any other country.   This has been due mainly to the existence of free trade in raw materials, which has made monopolisation of the home supplies impossible, and to our large dependence upon foreign sources of supply, few of which can be effectively monopolised.   Where attempts have been made to monopolise these sources, as in the case of rubber and of iron ore, vertical combinations have been formed of manufacturing firms in Great Britain and raw material suppliers abroad.   But since the need for self-protection has been far less acute than in Germany or in the United States, this form of combination has made little headway as yet. There is, however, some evidence that the various schemes of raw material control that have come into existence during the past two decades have led to some increase of combination in order to reduce the costs of the manufacturing firm.

§ 5. Lateral Integration. May I come finally to what has been called 'lateral integration'? This is the lateral expansion of firms neither in the direction of their existing main product, as with horizontal integration, nor in the direction of supplies and outlets, as with vertical integration, but in the direction of other different, but often broadly similar, activities. We find, for example, the English Electric Company making not only electric generating plant of normal types but expanding also into the design and building of nuclear power stations, the building of aircraft and aircraft engines and a range of other activities to which their scientific skill and managerial energies can be profitably applied. We find, again, firms like Hawker-Siddeley covering not only a wide range of activities in the aircraft industry but branching out also into other activities in the general field of engineering. We find Unilevers engaged not only in making soap but in making a number of products, including margarine, which derive ultimately from some of the same raw materials.

We have already seen many of the reasons, largely involved in methods of reconciling different optima, which may lead firms into this kind of integration. The arguments of risk-spreading are often, but not always, the principal ones. Sometimes, as was argued earlier, the reasons are concerned with the economies of selling a number of products through a single sales organisation. But largely also lateral integration is the direct consequence of change and uncertainty. One must conceive a firm in many typical industries as trying to plan its course of activities in a constantly changing world in which it produces a constantly changing series of products. It is everlastingly moving on from last year's designs to next year's. It is trying to find the gap in the national jig-saw of activities into which for the time being it can most neatly fit.

In the process of time the firm will have acquired certain fixed equipment, certain liquid resources, certain experience, certain good-will. But the products that it used to make may no longer command the same markets, or the same high prices in those markets, as they have done in the past. The firm, if it is alive and vigorous, will be feeling out and reinvesting in new and more profitable lines of activity where its experience, goodwill and resources can be used. But it will seldom wholly abandon its old activities. Thus the typical firm is often a multi-product firm, not only in the sense of producing together the variety of slightly differing designs which usually are sold together (as is customary, for example, in the case of boot and shoe manufacturers), but in the wider sense of having different departments concerned with basically different types of activity.

In addition to the forces that I have just mentioned there are other important factors causing or contributing to lateral integration. First among these I would put the possession of liquid capital. If a firm has made profits and possesses funds which (perhaps under official pressure) it does not wish to distribute to shareholders, it has various possible outlets: it may expand its existing activities; it may purchase investments; it may branch out, possibly by buying a subsidiary, into another field. A firm already on a fairly large scale in one market may decide not to increase its output in that market, if only for fear of spoiling it. It may prefer to use its resources to acquire and resuscitate a subsidiary or to build a new enterprise in a different but probably contiguous industry.

Second, I would put the possession of technical and organising 'know-how.' There are certain firms in Great Britain, as in the United States, which have succeeded in recruiting specialist staffs with outstanding competence in the solution of difficult new manufacturing and production problems, in the development of projects from the laboratory to the pilot plant and from the pilot plant to the final full scale plant, and in the design and construction of plants. Once production is established and the plant run in, such specialist staffs are no longer required to operate it. But they provide for that firm an unique advantage in tackling some other kindred problem. It is fascinating to watch the continuing lateral expansions of such firms, sometimes of their own volition, sometimes at the request of a government department, anxious to see some new import-saving activity introduced into the country.

§ **6. The Multi-Product Firm.** This constant process of change and adjustment to change, of risk-spreading, of making the most of selling economies, gives us the multi-product firm as we know it. We see it distributing its activities as best it can between products whose markets are declining and those whose markets are growing, between highly profitable but seasonal or intermittent markets and steady-selling but low-profit markets, expanding when times are good or exceptional opportunity offers, disposing of subsidiaries or closing down on certain activities when times are bad.

If we are interested principally in a description of what is, we can see and explain. If we are interested in what ought to be, it is much more difficult to pass judgment. I would myself regard some degree of lateral integration as inevitable and even desirable. But I would find it much more difficult in the light of American experience to justify anything like the extent of multiplicity which in fact exists in Britain to-day. Some of it is right and proper. Some of it appears to show an inability to calculate and pass on to the consumer the real costs of the marginal activities and varieties. Certainly progress in America has been associated with much more specialisation of plants on a narrow range of products than we ordinarily find in Britain. It is not easy to explain why that should be so. There are a few industries in which the very large American market permits, while ours does not permit, the reasonably easy achievement of optimum size and specialisation. But it is dangerous to write the whole of industrial economics in terms of the automobile industry; the evidence of the Censuses of Production and the researches of Professor Sargant Florence, Mr. Rostas and others have shown that in a large majority of industries British firms are no smaller, measured in terms of manpower employed, than American firms. The explanation would seem to lie more in the character of the American market, in the willingness of the American consumer to accept standardisation, and in the determination and power of the American producer and retailer to coerce him by sales pressure than in the straight and simple economies of mere size of the market.

CHAPTER IX

THE OPTIMUM INDUSTRY

§ 1. The Relation of Cost to the Scale of the Industry.
We have hitherto been engaged in considering how the cost of
production varies in firms of different sizes, and what is the
optimum size of the firm if the cost of production is to be at
a minimum.   But the cost of production will depend not only
upon the size of the firm, but also upon the number of firms
engaged together in producing the commodity.   For a number
of firms can secure economies which are not available to any
one of the firms individually.   There are many things which
a firm has to buy from outside its own walls, many organisations which are used in common by all the firms in the industry
that can operate more efficiently when the whole industry
which they are serving is on a larger scale.   We have already
considered the case of the specialist firm which carries off
from the main industry one particular process in order that it
may concentrate more narrowly upon this, and secure the
greatest economies of production.   It will get these greatest
economies only if the industry as a whole is sufficiently large
to give it the scale necessary for the greatest efficiency.   If it
needs a scale equal to producing for ten firms in the main
industry, and there are in fact only eight firms, a growth of
the whole industry will reduce the costs and probably also the
prices of this specialist firm, and so those of the whole
industry.   There are many other subsidiaries to the main
industry that will afford similar economies to the industry.
Thus as the industry grows, it is likely to buy more cheaply
the machinery that it employs, it is likely to enjoy opportunities of selling waste products to by-product firms, which

for a smaller industry would have been unprofitable. The several firms are likely to enjoy common advantages both of fundamental research and of practical solutions to the various technical problems which arise; more minds will be applied to the problems of the industry and solutions of its problems will be found which no one individual could have discovered. The firms will share the gains of a large specially skilled labour force. Transport and banking facilities will be available to the larger industry which would have been impossible or unprofitable with a smaller industry; organised markets both for the material of the industry and for the finished products of the industry may be expected to become more efficient the larger is the industry as a whole.

It is evident then that we have not exhausted all the available economies when we have reached the scale of production which will make possible one firm of optimum size. But if we attempt to measure these economies and to relate them to the growth of the output of the industry as a whole, as distinct from the individual firm, we discover almost at once a considerable difficulty in our analysis. For as we saw in the first chapter, it is by no means easy to define what we mean by a commodity. If we are to discuss the cost of production of a commodity, and how it is affected by the quantity of the commodity produced, we ought to start, if our thinking is to be clear, with some clearly defined conception of what is and what is not the commodity of which we are speaking. If we are talking about wheat or herrings, it may not be impossible, but if we are talking even about coal, difficulties begin to arise The Rhenish Westphalian Coal Cartel recognised over 1400 different types of coal. If we are talking about the chocolate trade, or the women's clothing trade, to attempt to treat the goods which they produce as if they constituted single homogeneous commodities is obviously ridiculous; but the very thing we want to consider is how far producing more, of whatever it may be that we are discussing, changes its cost of production, and if we cannot say whether more or less of a commodity is being produced, we cannot say very well whether producing more or less makes production cheaper or more expensive.

For these economies, the external economies as they are called to distinguish them from the internal economies which depend upon the size of the individual undertaking, depend only in part upon the quantity of the one particular commodity that is being turned out, and in part also upon the quantities of other commodities which for one reason or another share in certain of the costs of production of this particular commodity. If, for example, the output of certain types of women's ready-made clothing were to increase, the economies obtained and therefore the cost would depend very largely upon whether there was a simultaneous increase or decline in other parts of the trade which employ similar labour, similar machinery, similar distributing agencies and raw material sources. Many of these economies, that is to say, depend more upon the general volume of output of a group of allied commodities than upon the volume of output in one particular small section of a trade. A great deal of machinery, again, is common to a number of industries: three industries as different as cocoa, corn-flakes and detergents use the same equipment to fill and weigh their packages. Moreover the costs of the whole trade will depend to some extent upon the general development of industry in the producing country. Almost every trade uses structural steel, almost every trade employs the services of transport and of banking, and the price of these will depend upon the size of the market offered to them by the whole industry of the country.

§ 2. The Limits to Increases of Efficiency.

We saw in the case of the individual firm that as a firm grew, it secured certain economies, but in general the larger it grew, the less was likely to be the gain to be secured by further growth, the greater on the other hand the losses consequent upon that growth. In the same way, the larger an industry grows, the less are the economies to be secured by further growth, the greater in certain cases are the losses as the most advantageous sites and the most advantageous sources of materials are appropriated, and further firms have to depend on less advantageous sites and materials. For if we say that the main industry, let us take for instance the cotton industry, is enjoying diminishing costs as the result of external economies, we are in fact saying that the subsidiary industries or organisations are enjoying diminishing costs. These in their turn must be due either to internal or to external economies of the subsidiary industry. Either, that is, they arise through a firm or organisation being below its optimum scale, or from something external to that firm or organisation. Either the cotton machinery industry is enjoying internal economies through the specialist firms being each below their optimum capacity, or the economy is external again to the cotton machinery industry. And so we chase this will-o'-the-wisp of external economy through industry after industry, and we find it vanishing in the end or absorbed in the economies of firms or organisations below their optimum capacity.

As an industry grows, therefore, the gains from further growth gradually disappear until that industry has reached its optimum scale. If the industry depends in large degree upon factors of production of which a given quality is limited in amount, as for example upon minerals, or upon water supplies, diseconomies are likely to arise progressively as the industry in one area expands, until the growing diseconomies outweigh the further economies to be secured by growth. In such cases the optimum industry, concentrated in any one country, or in any one area, may be comparatively small. Where, on the other hand, the final product and the raw materials are alike easily transportable, the optimum industry is likely to be far greater, and the limit to its efficient size will be set, not by gradually increasing diseconomies, but by the increasing transport costs as more distant markets come to be served. Thus the optimum industry is itself in part determined by the location of consumers.

Let us try now to measure, so far as it is at all possible, the gains which can be expected from some of these external economies. We can start our inquiry from a platitude. A greater amount of a product cannot cost less in aggregate to produce than a smaller amount. If this were not true, the cheapest way of producing the smaller amount would be to produce the larger amount. It is impossible that by doubling the output of motor cars, the cost of each car should be more than halved; if it were so, the cheapest way of producing the smaller number of cars would be to produce the larger number, and drive half of them over a cliff into the sea. Of course it is quite impossible that the economy should be anything like so great as this, since it will always be necessary to buy raw materials for the larger quantity which would be unnecessary for the smaller, but it is clear that this will give us an upper limit to our possible economies.

Let us take a single example, and see how big our external economies are likely to be. Since transport is common to all industries, that will afford a suitable illustration. The total number of persons engaged in transport in this country is about 7 per cent of the whole occupied male population. The cost of transport is estimated as representing between 10 per cent and 15 per cent of the cost of all export goods. Let us for purposes of argument regard the cost of transport as equal to 10 per cent of the cost of all goods, then we can say that the upper limit of the possible economies from transport, if the national output were doubled, would be an economy of 5 per cent. For if transport represents 10 per cent of the present dividend, it cannot represent less than 5 per cent of the doubled dividend, which is equivalent to a saving of 5 per cent. But in fact the possible saving cannot be of this magnitude; for some part of the expenditure of the railways is directly dependent on the amount of traffic carried. The labour of loading or unloading wagons, the repair of wagons and rolling stock, the consumption of coal, at least in part vary with the quantity of the goods carried. Let us suppose that for a doubling of the traffic carried, these items were increased by only 50 per cent, then, since they represent about 50 per cent of the total expenditure of a railway company, the total expenditure will have increased about 25 per cent. That is to say, the proportion of all the expenses of production represented by transport would, on my more or less hypothetical assumptions, have fallen not to 5 per cent but to $6\frac{1}{4}$ per cent of the larger national dividend. The possible saving would therefore be under 4 per cent, and the saving which we might expect to achieve in practice would almost certainly be very much less.

This somewhat elaborate calculation has been made because economists all too frequently draw diagrams which imply rates of diminishing cost which could not possibly be realised in practice. Even inside the individual firm, it must always remain true that the larger quantity cannot cost less than the smaller quantity, and since raw materials frequently represent 50 per cent of the total cost, and they are not open to very considerable economies of purchase with increases of output, the realisable rate of diminishing cost is generally small. Where the costs diminish through external economies, the rate of diminution is likely to be even smaller. For in general, the external economies apply to a comparatively small proportion of the total costs of an industry.

We have, of course, been forced to assume in this discussion that there is no great and sudden change in the technique of production. When we were discussing the possible economies of railway transport, we assumed that the same methods were employed for the larger volume of transport as for the smaller volume, except in so far as the larger volume made possible and profitable methods which were impossible and unprofitable for the smaller volume. But where the larger volume made a change of technique or of organisation profitable, we assumed it to be employed. Now, in economic analysis, it is easy enough to distinguish these economies which are the consequence of the increased output from inventions which could have been applied equally with the older, smaller output. In real life, however, this rigid distinction is extremely difficult. Few of us would care to say how far the British cotton industry or the American motor industry has owed its superiority over its rivals to methods and technique which are only applicable with the outputs of Lancashire or of Detroit, and how far, on the other hand, the superiority has been due to the earlier or more intelligent use of methods which would have been equally applicable with a smaller output. But if we wish to say anything practical concerning the relation of output to cost, whether inside the firm or inside the industry, this distinction must be made. For unless we can make it, we cannot possibly say, for example, whether a large motor industry is or is not the condition of cheap production, and whether or not there is a real prospect of establishing in this country an industry of efficiency comparable to that of the American motor industry.

§ 3. The Mobility of Economies. But this brings us to a further complication. We may divide external economies into mobile and immobile economies. There are certain external economies which you must go and fetch for yourself; there are others which will come to you. Specialist firms in Manchester who will pack cotton goods are almost useless to a mill owner in Central India. Yet that same mill owner can and does share the advantage of the Liverpool cotton market. He hedges as easily and conveniently as his rival in Oldham. He shares also, to a large extent, the advantages of machinery improvement, of better dyes, of research into methods of using the shorter Indian cottons. These economies may come to him later than to his Lancashire rival, but the period of advantage is constantly shortening.

We can see then that certain external economies, though by no means all, depend not on the size of the industry in one locality, but on the size of that industry in the world as a whole. We can, I think, say that the proportion of all economies which are of this international mobile type is steadily increasing, and that the advantage of a large industry concentrated in one country is steadily declining as the mobility of economies increases; that is, that the optimum local industry is diminishing in size. But this leads us into yet another difficulty. It would appear that the best world distribution of industry is a high degree of concentration in one place with a number of other sub-concentrations living parasitically upon the main concentration. So long as the main concentration persists, these sub-concentrations can depend on it for development of machinery, of technique, and of fundamental research, and so long as they can depend upon it their efficiency may not be considerably lower, in certain circumstances their costs may even be less, than those of the main concentration. But if the main concentration were to break down, the sub-concentrations might find themselves unable to supply their own needs. It is clear that the extent to which a failure of the main concentration (let us take as an example the Lancashire cotton industry) would affect the sub-concentrations would depend upon the relations between the sources of the localised external economies and the main concentration. For the Liverpool cotton market, on the one hand, and the makers of cotton machinery, on the other, are likely to be affected in different degrees by the decline of the local industry. The market would be likely to be weakened almost proportionately; the machinery industry might survive for some time the removal of its consuming firms to other centres, but it is likely that, in the long run, machinery will be best produced where a large number of persons are giving their minds to the current technical problems of the industry.

It will be gathered from the preceding paragraphs that there is no easy or simple general answer to the question of the optimum size of an industry. The answer will depend first upon the extent of the dependence of the individual firms upon common specialist firms and common organisations. As these reach their several optimum scales, further economies disappear. The answer will depend also on the mobility of these economies, how far they can be shared by firms outside the particular district or country in which the economies arise, and, finally, upon how far those economies would disappear if at least one large concentration of production did not exist. We can see therefore that the practical politician who wishes to make judgments concerning the fostering or the exposure of new-born infant industries must first make all sorts of assumptions concerning the future concentrations of production in many other countries, assumptions which even political gifts of prophecy may find at times a trifle difficult.

CHAPTER X

THE LOCATION OF PRODUCTION
(1) NATIONAL

§ **1. Costs of Transport and Location.** We have already seen that a limit to the division of labour, and to growth towards the optimum scale of production, is set in many instances by the size of the local market. We must now proceed to consider this limitation, and the extent to which it can be evaded by the action of an intelligent entrepreneur. It is clear that the area and population of the available market will depend in part at least upon the selection of that location for the firm which will afford the most ready access to the whole market to be served, and that the size of the individual firm will depend upon the radius of the circle within which it can profitably distribute its goods, and upon the density of the population living within that circle. It is therefore the problem of industrial localisation that we have to consider, in particular in its relation to the size of the individual firm.

The factors which influence the choice of a place of production fall into two broad groups; first the factors which determine where the transport costs involved will be at a minimum, second the factors which make for lower costs of production at some places than at other places. We will consider first the effect of transport costs on the location of firms, assuming for the time being that costs of production are everywhere the same. All commodities, as distinct from services, must have at least two points of attachment to the earth's surface, a place of consumption of the finished commodity, and a place of origin of a raw material. Let us start from the simplest possible case, in which a single market

127

and a single material are alone involved, as they are for instance in the making of gas. The place of production will be either at the source of material or at the place of consumption, according as the material or the finished article is the more expensive to carry.

It is likely to be at the source of material if the material is more expensive to carry than the finished product. This is likely to be the case wherever the finished product embodies comparatively little of the weight of the raw materials employed in its manufacture. Thus a ton of aluminium can be produced only by the working of many tons of clay, and the use of large quantities of water. The coal employed in heating glass furnaces is not incorporated in the weight of the finished sheets of glass.

Production is likely to be at the place of consumption where the final product is more expensive to carry, because it is more bulky, more fragile, or more perishable than its raw materials, as it is in the extreme case of houses, in the more normal instances of cakes, of ice, of fitted shelves. The finished product itself cannot, of course, weigh more than the materials of which it is made; but with packing included it can sometimes do so, and when, as for the calculation of shipping freight, weight is measured by cubic content it can often do so. It is at the place of consumption also where the finished product is only slightly more expensive to carry than the materials, but embodies the whole, or practically the whole, of the materials employed in its manufacture. Cotton and wool may be carried to their markets for manufacture because they lose but little of their weight in transformation into consumable commodities.

In the more complex instances, where several materials are combined into a single commodity, a predominant weight-losing material is still likely to attract production to itself, but where two materials, both losing considerable weight in process of production, are required, the actual place of production may be in some cases at the source of one of these materials, in other cases at a place between the two with opportunities

of access to the market. The iron and steel industry provides
an interesting example of the effects of two such materials.
The industry in this country is to be found on the North-
East Coast at a point where both foreign and local supplies
of ore are available, with convenient access to coal; in
Scotland at the coal, in South Wales sometimes at the coal,
but more often now at the coast, employing imported ore;
on the North-West Coast again at the coal, employing partly
local, partly imported ore; in Lincolnshire at the ore supplies,
using coal or coke brought from a distance. In this case,
the best location depends entirely upon the richness of the
ore to be worked. With rich ore containing 50 per cent to
70 per cent of metal, the coal required is about equal in
weight to the ore; with the poorer ores, containing about 30
per cent of metal, about two tons of ore have to be used for
every ton of coal. The industry is likely, therefore, to be
found at the coal where rich ores, and imported ores are
mostly rich ores, are used. It is likely to be at the ore
supply where, as in Lincolnshire and Cleveland, low grade
ores are in use. But changes in the technical methods of
an industry which made possible an economy of fuel might
alter completely the most economical place of production.
The gradual change from heavy fuel consumption and rich iron
ores to lower fuel consumption and poorer ores has brought
about a remarkable change in the location of the processes
of the industry, reinforced in certain respects by the changed
technique of coke and by-product manufacture, and the
increasing use of coking oven gas in the manufacture of steel.

So far, we have regarded the problem as that of combining
two or more materials, each available at a known spot, to
provide a supply for a known place of consumption. In
practice it is not always immediately apparent from which
of several sources each of the raw materials can most conveniently be drawn. Is the clay for bricks to be used in
Cambridge to be drawn from the nearest clay pit to Cambridge, the coal necessary being brought to it from the coalfield, or is the clay nearest the coalfield to be used, and the

bricks carried from the coalfield to Cambridge? We cannot lay down any quite certain answer to this problem, except by examining each particular case, but there is one thing that can be said. If a raw material were available everywhere, then the place of production would be fixed independently of it, and the material would be used at the spot which was fixed by other considerations. Where a material is available very widely, as is brick clay in most countries, or timber in some countries, it may be very nearly accurate to regard the place of production as fixed independently of this material.

Between the limits of the absolutely fixed material and the completely ubiquitous material, there are many other materials which are displaceable, but displaceable at a cost. Certain crops can if necessary be grown in almost any area, but certain areas are more suitable than others. The silts round Boston grow the best potatoes; the black cotton soil of India, the delta lands of the Mississippi, the Nile, and the Ganges, have all peculiar advantages for their special crops. Even resources which are normally ubiquitous may so vary in quantity or quality that they are in fact best regarded as fixed for certain purposes. For ordinary industrial purposes water may be had anywhere, but when very great quantities are required for bleaching, for cooling the condensers of large electrical generating stations, or driving the turbines themselves, the few adequate sources of supply are limited and fixed. 'Why was Burton built on Trent?' The peculiar properties of the waters of Burton provide the prosaic answer to the poetical question. These fixed, semi-fixed and ubiquitous materials attract production towards themselves with a pull which depends in part, as we have seen, on the extent to which they lose their weight in entering into the finished product, in part on the extent to which their source of supply can, at a cost, be changed.

Coal, absolutely fixed, losing its whole weight in production, possesses a unique power of attracting production, and the nineteenth century location of industry was built in this country almost entirely upon coal. The possibility of converting it on a large scale into electricity has made it in recent years somewhat more portable, but so long as interest must be paid upon the capital expended in constructing the inter-connecting grid, power will continue to be not vastly more transportable than many raw materials. But whereas the extra cost of carrying each extra ton of coal in trucks on railways must be almost as high as the carriage of each exist-ing ton, the extra cost of transmitting further current on transmission lines not at present worked to their full capacity may be very low indeed. Some shift from location at the coal towards location at raw materials, at the market, or at the port of entry may therefore be expected, but it must be remembered that most industries which require power on a large scale use coal also for the provision of heat in the processes of production, and that electricity can less easily and economically be substituted for the direct use of coal for this purpose.

§ 2. The Influence of Cheap Supplies of Factors of Production. These various forces, pulling the point of production towards the raw materials on the one hand, towards the place of con-sumption on the other, may be regarded as tending to establish at some place a point of minimum total transport cost.[1] This is not necessarily the most desirable place of production, for we have already seen that certain economies may be available at other points. Labour may be cheaper or more efficient, materials better or more easily workable, manufacturing economies may be obtainable by moving to some other point; but these economies will be worth pursuing only if the economy exceeds the cost of obtaining it, and that cost is measured by the increase of transport cost involved in pro-ducing at some point other than that which gives the minimum total transport cost. It is evident that the economy necessary

[1] A mechanical model for the determination of this point has been suggested by Alfred Weber (*Theory of Location of Industries*, English Edition, p. 229), from whose work many of the ideas in this chapter have been derived.

to divert production from the point of minimum transport cost must be great in those commodities in which transport cost is high.

The economies which are pursued in this way arise from cheap supplies of any of the factors of production. Thus cheap land, cheap labour, cheap capital, efficient business management, may all attract production from other places where their prices are higher. In recent years a movement of factories from the centres of towns into the outskirts has become common. The purpose of the move has in most cases been that room for expansion in cheap single-storeyed buildings may be found. Cheap labour, however, probably exercises more influence on the location of the easily movable industries than any other single factor. The history of such towns as Coventry has shown that a supply of skilled labour accustomed to factory work will attract new industries as the old decay. Coventry has been at different periods the centre of a flourishing woollen trade, of a manufacture of ribbons, of watches, cycles, motor cars. In other instances, an industry has been retained by a town chiefly because the skilled labour of the industry has been concentrated there. It is probably the skill of Lancashire as much at its notoriously humid climate which holds the cotton industry.

Capital and business management are generally more mobile than the other factors that we have considered, and tend therefore to move towards them rather than to attract them. Cheap capital, however, exercises some considerable influence in regard to the international location of industries, and must not be entirely forgotten. Business management occasionally succeeds in attracting production to itself; where it succeeds, the spur seems to be that of sentiment more often than of economics. Mr. Ford started to manufacture motor cars in Detroit because it was his home town. Lord Nuffield selected Cowley because the school in which his father was educated happened to be for sale. Neither of these excellent motives can be regarded as promising certain success to those who imitate them. Mr. Ford and Lord Nuffield could probably have succeeded anywhere; humbler men must be wise or fail. Their failure may serve to bring one important point to our notice. The location of industry is not solely the consequence of thought, it is the consequence also of a certain competitive selection. Motor firms spring up like grass after Indian rains; they die almost as quickly. They survive only if they have wisely chosen their methods, their designs and their location. If more survive at Coventry and Birmingham than in other places, it is some indication that those two cities possess advantages for the industry. Mr. Ford and Lord Nuffield, either by acumen or by chance, discovered places of production with great natural advantages. At Cowley, for purposes of assembly, as distinct from manufacture (which is, in fact, carried on chiefly in Coventry and Birmingham), large supplies of efficient, energetic, but not exceptionally highly skilled labour are required. The cream of the Oxfordshire agricultural population, not yet skimmed by rival industries, was here available when Lord Nuffield first started; labour has more recently been attracted from all over the country. Thus, though Lord Nuffield's original decision may have been influenced partly by sentiment, his choice has been fully justified by the event.

§ 3. **Large Scale Production and Location.** At the start of this study of industrial location, we were forced to assume that materials from certain sources were being employed to serve a single known market. But in practice it is obvious that very few towns now require the entire services of a single firm of optimum size. We have therefore to see how far the economies of large scale operation react upon the location of individual firms. We can imagine two separate markets, each deriving its supply of the raw materials of a given commodity from the same source; each of these markets will have its own point of lowest aggregate transport costs, which will necessarily in a theoretical world be slightly different (in a practical world the hard facts of the alignment of railway tracks or other possible avenues of transport may make them identical); we have to consider in what circumstances it will be profitable to combine these two separate points of production into one point.   Let us for simplicity assume that one only is to move.   The inhabitants of Downham will get their bread from the bakery at Upham if they can get it cheaper by doing so.   If therefore the gain in efficiency through spreading certain overhead costs over a larger output, or through introducing new methods which were unprofitable with the smaller output, is sufficient to offset the cost of carrying the loaves down the hill, the baker of Upham will undersell his rival and the two village bakeries will be combined into one.   We must see in exactly what circumstances it will be profitable to combine the two.   The condition is not, as might be supposed, that the average cost of each loaf at Upham, when all the bread for both villages is produced there, shall be less than the average cost of each loaf at Downham by an amount sufficient to pay for its cartage down the hill.   The condition is rather that the extra cost of producing at Upham the loaves required at Downham, in addition to the output required for Upham, should be less than the cost of producing that quantity of loaves in an independent bakery at Downham, by an amount sufficient to pay for their cartage. The baker is already, we may presume, covering his overhead costs by his sales at Upham; if therefore the loaves he sells at Downham more than cover the extra cost of materials and an adequate return on the slight extra capital involved, he will be receiving an addition to profits which may perhaps be passed on to the inhabitants of Upham in cheaper bread, so that the inhabitants of Upham may also be better off as the result of the combination.   The baker will therefore be able to sell bread for Downham cheaper than he can sell bread for Upham, but he will not find it worth while to sell his loaves so much cheaper at Downham than at Upham that the people of Upham will ask a friend at Downham to take in a loaf for them.   He will as a rule in practice charge the same price at both places, but deliver his bread free to Downham; this is in effect to charge the people of Downham less by the amount of the cartage.

This illustration helps us to understand the circumstances in which production will be concentrated into certain centres. Concentration will proceed up to the point where the marginal cost of making the marginal unit of output at a centre of concentration, together with the greater cost of carrying the goods to the market, is equal to the greater marginal cost at a point of less concentration nearer to the market with a lower or no cost of carrying the goods. We may distinguish conveniently two stages of concentration. First a concentration in order that single firms each working in their own markets may achieve their optimum scale of production, second a further concentration in order that many firms operating in a limited area may share immobile external economies. It is evident that this second degree of concentration can take place only where the costs of transport are such a small proportion of the whole that the place of production is cheaply diverted.

§ 4. **Degrees of Industrial Concentration.**   In different industries, the degree of concentration normally achieved is markedly different. Where, because of fragility, perishability, or bulk, the finished goods are costly to transport, the normal concentration is likely to be low. The unit of baking, of building, of ice manufacture is small not because economies of large scale production do not exist, but because transport costs or transport difficulties prevent concentration of the industry into large units. In this connection, it is interesting to contrast the milling industries of the United States and of this country. In the United States, the industry is carried on by small firms, employing in 1919 an average of under five men, milling (in most cases) locally grown grain for local markets; in Great Britain, the industry is mainly in the hands of three large and recently rationalised firms, which carry on the industry at the ports of entry of the grain with the latest and most elaborate plant.

Concentration approaching the scale of the optimum firm is less easy to discover than the purely local industry on the one hand, the industry localised entirely in one town or region on the other. It would appear that this degree of concentration normally prevails in book printing, in electrical and agricultural engineering, in food processing, in brewing and in oil refining, to take only a few examples. Other examples of this tendency can be discovered in the somewhat analogous retail trades. The local draper is giving place to the more efficient large town draper faster, in most cases, than the latter is losing trade to the more highly localised London stores. The large town drapery store can secure most of the economies of large scale in large purchases, and a large choice of goods, in particular if it is one of a chain of similar stores. Thus we would expect to find the shops in the larger market towns expanding towards their optimum size by absorbing the custom of the small village shop.

Proceeding further up the scale, we find industries which are almost wholly localised in a single area. Cotton, wool, cutlery, boots and shoes are all confined in the main to their own fairly well defined districts. Within these districts, special external economies and specially skilled labour are available to them. Some of these external economies are economies of concentration, others arise from advantages of location, and we must distinguish these two influences. It is possible that an industry should be concentrated at some point as the result of historical causes and that it should enjoy there all the economies of concentration, but that the point of concentration should be a point other than the most desirable point of concentration having regard to present sources of raw materials and present technical methods of production. The concentration of the potteries in Staffordshire is largely the result of their historical development; it is quite possible that, if the whole concentration could be magically transferred to some spot nearer to the deposits of china clay that are at present being used, the costs of the industry could be considerably reduced, but so long as the industry remains concentrated in Staffordshire, it is to the interest of any new firm to start there rather than at the clay supplies.

§ 5. The Influence of the Market.

We have hitherto treated the market as if it were known and fixed. It is important to remember that the position of the market itself is in large measure a consequence of the location of industry. Its position to-day is very different from its position before the industrial revolution. Some 60 per cent of the population lives to-day within the six chief industrial areas of the country, drawn there by the needs of industry. Other sections of the community are equally located by the location of industry in that they seek for the places which have escaped industrialism. Bournemouth, Brighton, Blackpool, St. Andrews, attract those who seek to escape from the consequences of industry, but their location is more fickle, less narrowly economic than the location of Sheffield, Manchester, Middlesbrough or Birmingham. A movement of these accidental centres would nevertheless affect the whole structure that is built in part upon them. But part only of industry depends upon the accidents of courts and kings and fashions, of grouse and golf balls and gallops. The industries which export dhotis or structural steel or football boots through known ports to known markets have within this country a more certainly fixed location that those which minister to the ever-changing dictates of fashion. But any initial shift causes many secondary movements. The shift from south and east to the north in the industrial revolution, the shift back from north to south in recent years, has shifted not only the place of certain manufactures, but also the places of consumption to which many further industries are ministering, and has thus reinforced the initial movement.

CHAPTER XI

THE LOCATION OF PRODUCTION
(2) INTERNATIONAL

§ 1. The Assumption of Immobility. In the last chapter we were concerned with the location of firms and industries inside a single country. We saw that even within a country, labour supplies which were cheap, either because for a standard wage efficiency was higher, or because for a given efficiency money wages were lower, might attract the point of production. Inequalities of efficiency wages can continue to exist only where there is immobility of labour, so that workers in the lower paid area do not move to the higher paid area. Such immobility may be the result either of ignorance, which might with advantage be enlightened, or of costs of movement which cannot profitably be overcome. The resistance to movement will, as a rule, be greatest when it entails a movement across a political and linguistic frontier. In this case the resistance may be so great that immobility of labour is a more reasonable assumption than mobility of labour. A similar, but somewhat less powerful, resistance to mobility will be found to exist also in the case of the controllers of business enterprise, and a very much less powerful resistance in the case of capital.

§ 2. The International Division of Labour. Where the assumption of immobility is more accurate than the assumption of mobility, we can work out a theory of industrial location on that assumption. Since it applies more generally to the international location of industry, it is known as a rule as the 'theory of international trade.' This theory, despite its high-

138

sounding name, is nothing new or unfamiliar. It is merely the extension into the field of international trading of the general principle of the gains of specialisation and division of labour that we discussed in their relation to the individual in the second chapter. We saw there that, by specialising on the work that they are best fitted to do, men and women can increase the volume of things which they have for their consumption and enjoyment. If everyone does that which he is individually best fitted to do, the totality of things will be greatest.

Sir Winston Churchill is, we are told, an excellent bricklayer, but he is a still more admirable author and politician. We are probably better off, and certainly better entertained, when Sir Winston makes all the speeches and an anonymous local bricklayer builds the wall, than if Sir Winston Churchill and the bricklayer each built half the wall and made half the speeches. This is not necessarily a disparagement of Sir Winston's bricklaying; it would be true even if he was an unusually competent bricklayer, for the qualities of a politician are rarer and more highly rewarded than those of a bricklayer. Even were one man more efficient at everything than anyone else, this paragon ought not to be self-sufficient. His talents would be better used if wholly devoted to ruling his country, or to writing books, than if partly employed for the perfect dusting of rooms and the superlative making of beds. Exchange between the efficient and the inefficient will be beneficial to both parties. It is as much to the advantage of the incompetent to do that work in which incompetence makes least difference, as to that of the expert to concentrate on his specialised function.

The principles which govern the international location of industry are but a development of these simple truisms. In the same way that a group of individuals may gain by specialisation, a group of nations may also gain by specialisation. If we attempted laboriously to grow oranges and bananas and coconuts for ourselves, and left the inhabitants of those countries which now produce them to build their own ships and motor cars and dynamos, the world would be a much poorer place than it is to-day. As it is, we import them, and export our products in exchange.

The things which we import may, if we like, be divided into two broad classes. First, we import those things which we cannot produce for ourselves: diamonds, certain ores, raw cotton, tobacco, tea, coffee, and those foreign wares, like Parisian dresses and Persian carpets, part of whose attraction is derived from their origin. Second, we import things which foreigners can make more cheaply than we can, and send to us as their most efficient products in exchange for the things they take from us. The gain from international division of labour, like that from the division between individuals, arises from the differences between the comparative efficiencies of different people or different nations at different sorts of work. If each nation were equally adapted to every industry, and there were no gains from large scale industry, there would be no gain from international trade. It is because the quantity of cotton that can be grown by the number of workers required to make a motor car is widely different in Coventry and in Central India or Uganda that trade between the two is profitable. There is reason to think that the specialisation which is desirable will in fact be brought about in most cases by the free play of economic and financial forces. Prices, wage levels and exchange rates in different countries will tend to be such that just sufficient exporting industry is located in each country to pay for the existing volume of imports. Such adjustment may be at times somewhat slow and painful, but when achieved it will secure the greatest flow of income to both parties to the trade.

§ 3. The Problem of Interference. We must now start on a path which, though well trodden, is yet still beset with the thorns and brambles of political controversy. We want to know in what conditions we may with advantage interfere to alter by protection or by subsidy the naturally determined location of industries. We must start with a strong presumption against interference. We have seen that there will be a tendency for countries to find themselves engaged in those industries in which the particular resources and qualities which they possess can be most profitably employed. If we are to show that interference is justified, we must show that business men, in the pursuit of their own profits, do not necessarily embark on those enterprises which are also most profitable to the country.

There is one fundamental difficulty which we must face immediately. The free play of economic forces will, apart from a few exceptional cases, make the economic welfare of the whole world greater in the long run than any alternative arrangement of resources. But as Britons, or Germans, or Americans, we may, rightly or wrongly, be concerned not with the wealth of the world, but with the wealth of an individual nation. In this case, it is sometimes possible that a single country, by acting as monopolist of its resources, might increase its own national wealth while diminishing by a greater amount the wealth of other nations. By limiting its imports, and therefore the volume of exports required to pay for them, it might so alter the terms of exchange that it received a larger share of the total gain from the trade. To decide whether in fact the conditions do exist in which the gain to be so secured in this way will exceed the losses incurred in other ways, is not always a very easy task.

Apart from this possibility, an excessive share of the resources of a country can be devoted to export trades only if employers in the export trades are paying, for some reason or other, less than the full cost to society of the resources which they are using. Thus it might be argued that in this country workers, when unemployed, are paid allowances either from an insurance scheme or by the Government. If the premiums of the insurance or the taxes of the Government are drawn equally from employers and workers in all industries, but more is paid out to workers in the more fluctuating industries, a subsidy is being paid by employers and workers in less fluctuating industries to employers and workers in more

11—s.c.i.

fluctuating industries. If, as there is reason to think, the fluctuations of employment are greater in the exporting industries than in the average of all industries, it might be argued that there is some subsidy to exporting industries, and that excessive resources tend therefore to be devoted to exporting.

§ 4. Infant Industries.   There is one condition in which it is generally agreed that interference may be desirable.   We saw in the last chapter that it was possible that an industry should be concentrated at one point which for the moment gave the greatest economies of concentration; but that if the industry could be bodily removed to another spot, and a new concentration developed there, the new centre would be more efficient than the old.   That problem may arise either within a single country or as between two centres in different countries.   If it can be shown that a new industry, if fostered and acclimatised for a few years, will be comparatively more efficient than that industry in other centres, and that the available resources of the country can secure a greater return by being devoted to that industry than to the best alternative use, it may be profitable so to foster it.   But it will only be profitable to foster it if the long period gain exceeds the short period loss.   In the same way, if one particular centre of an industry has declined temporarily from some eradicable cause, it may be profitable to nurse it for a time, if those same conditions of comparative efficiency are fulfilled.   These two arguments for temporary protection we may call 'the infant industry argument' and 'the invalid industry argument.' They apply, it must be always remembered, not to all infants and to all invalids, but to infant prodigies and to wounded heroes.

§ 5. The Employment Argument.   An argument for temporary protection, somewhat similar in that it weighs future against immediate gains and losses, is that which finds its origin in the existence of unemployed and unused resources at home. You were perhaps a little worried about Sir Winston and his wall. If it took all Sir Winston's time and energy to write books and speeches, the argument was valid enough. But perhaps after he finished his literary labours for the day, he found time for building. If so, the world had a wall the more, and no less of literature. In much the same way, it may be argued that if a country has idle resources, and in particular idle labour, which must in any case be fed and clothed by the rest of the nation, it is better to employ it to make things than to go on buying those same things from abroad.

It is, of course, obvious that if we buy less from abroad our export trades will suffer to some extent. How much they will suffer will depend on the actual circumstances and must always be hard to predict. If, as in some conditions is likely, it is possible to reduce imports without an exactly corresponding decrease of exports, so that there is a temporary gain of employment, there will be almost certainly a more permanent loss arising from the maldistribution of resources. We have to balance these one against the other, and find whether the loss is so great that the temporary gain cannot possibly be held to offset it, or whether the long period loss is so moderate that a considerable immediate gain could be held sufficient to justify it. The problem we have to answer is whether in the case that we are considering the diversion of resources from the indirect manufacture of some of our imports, by production of exports and exchange, to the direct manufacture of those imports, will result in the long run in a considerable or only in a trifling reduction of the flow of goods which will be available for our consumption.

§ 6. The Key Industry Argument.   This problem has a further interest for us. Many of those who desire to protect individual industries, for reasons other than purely private gain, wish to do so because they regard a certain industry as desirable in itself, as a proper possession of any considerable country, or a necessary precaution against the risks of war.

Agriculture, or the iron and steel industry, or the chemical industry, is for them more than a means to wealth. They would be willing to sacrifice wealth in order to buy its presence in this country.

§ 7. The Cost of Protection. If we are to answer their arguments, we must be prepared to say not only that to keep agriculture alive by protection will make us poorer, but also that it will make us poorer by a greater amount than we can afford. Let us then make some attempt to measure the loss. By diverting resources we have affected two industries. We have made the exporting industry smaller, we have made the new protected industry larger; we may perhaps have brought it into existence. The damage which we inflict will depend, where the industries are already in existence, upon whether we have reduced the exporting industry below the scale of an optimum concentration of that industry, and whether the industry which we have fostered is below the scale of an optimum industry. The conditions which govern the optimum concentration of an industry were set out in an earlier chapter. It was there argued that there was reason to think that external economies were becoming more mobile, and that the optimum concentration of an industry was not in every case very large. If an ill-devised system of protection destroys this mobility of external economies, the optimum concentration may be very large, and the damage inflicted correspondingly great.

The damage inflicted will depend secondly, as we saw earlier, upon the difference of the relative efficiencies of the trading countries in producing the exported and imported goods. Where the ease of producing goods depends upon climate, or upon supplies of natural resources, the relative efficiency of labour and capital applied to two different industries may be widely different in two different countries. The number of bananas that could be produced by the labour required to build a locomotive would be widely different in Scotland and in the Canary Islands. But as regards a fairly considerable range of standard machine-produced products, it may be doubted whether the differences of relative efficiency are great. Goods are made in different countries with the help of almost identical machinery. Labour which is 80 per cent as efficient as our labour in operating boot and shoe machinery is likely to be about 80 per cent as efficient also in operating textile machinery or in machining motor parts. It is not particularly likely to be twice as efficient in one industry, half as efficient in another industry. In these industries, so long as raw material supplies are not of such different cost as to be of importance, the gain from specialisation is likely to be small, and to be the consequence rather of temporary differences of wage rates than of more fundamental differences of efficiency. The damage therefore which would arise from impeding the trade is likely to be not so considerable that it cannot in any circumstances be offset by gains. These gains may be either such gains as arise from an immediate reduction of unemployment, or the more long period and less easily assessable gains which may be held to result from a balance of industries, or a civilisation based upon a wide range of opportunity for individual activity.

We have seen that in certain isolated cases, it may sometimes be true that interference with the natural location of industry may make an individual country temporarily or even permanently richer. To suggest that because this may sometimes be the case, it is better to interfere always and everywhere is folly. It is worse, in fact, than folly. In its functions as a remedy of unemployment, protection can help, if at all, only in the act of being imposed. It is an iron ration which can be used but once; to consume it, therefore, before the moment of emergency, is suicidal. To suggest that it is better to interfere nowhere is a policy of caution that may bring its adherents nearer to the true course than a policy of indiscriminate interference, but is necessarily, in certain circumstances, a policy of accepting something worse than the best possible.

CHAPTER XII

INTERVENTION TO IMPROVE EFFICIENCY

§ 1. **The Scope of Intervention.** In the last chapter we were concerned for the first time with the problem of interference with the free play of economic forces in order to bring about an increase of welfare, either in a single country or in the world as a whole. In this chapter we must proceed to study the same problem more closely, from the point of view this time not of re-allocating industrial activities between different nations, but from the aspect of altering and improving industrial structure within a single country. The term 'rationalisation' was invented in the late 1920s to express this idea of semi-compulsory reorganisation, and for lack of a better modern term I shall continue to use it. It is with the nature of genuine rationalisation that I shall be concerned. The word has been defined in many senses, and everyone is, I suppose, free to use it in the sense that he wishes, provided that he makes his own definition clear. But it adds to the simplicity of life if we all give to the word much the same meaning, and I shall, I think, be following the best earlier precedents if I apply it only to the reorganisation of the relationship of the individual firm to the industry as a whole. I should distinguish it, therefore, from 'industrial efficiency,' or 'scientific management,' or internal reorganisation under any other name, which finds its field within the walls of the factory. My chief concern will be with the problem whether by some degree of interference we can make firms and combinations of firms of better form and size to achieve the maximum economies of production and marketing than that which they will automatically reach under conditions of non-interference.

We must begin by recalling briefly the forces which influence those who control a firm in deciding whether or not growth is desirable. They will take account, we have seen, of any further technical economies to be obtained by growth; they will consider whether they can efficiently manage and finance a large unit. They will examine its adaptability to permanent and temporary fluctuations of demand. Above all, they will have to consider whether, if they produce more, they can sell it without such an increase of sales costs as will eliminate the whole gain in other respects. We have seen how this increase of sales costs will differ according as growth takes the form of expansion or of combination, and that there may be a gain from growth by combination when there is no gain to be secured from growth by expansion.

But even if, when this calculation has been made, it shows a balance of advantage on the side of combination, it is by no means certain that combination will in fact take place. For combination is not an automatic consequence of the existence of a gain from combination. It is the result of a decision by those who are for the moment controlling a firm. But the gain of combination may arise in no small part from the elimination of those very individuals in whose hands the decision as to combination must lie. Thus the quick achievement of the most efficient technical unit must depend in many cases, not on the interest, but on the public spirit of individuals. In a longer period, combination by some producers, or the existence of more efficient units abroad, may, it is true, drive firms through the bankruptcy court into combination. But for a considerable interval it may happen that firms, which might profitably combine, do not in fact combine, either because those who are at present in control know that they will be eliminated, or because they prefer ownership of a small unit to a subordinate position in a larger unit.

One purpose of a scheme of rationalisation, then, may be to overcome the resistances of individual employers to the establishment of optimum units of production. There is often a second purpose. It is hoped, by a scheme of rationalisation, to concentrate production in those works which are best equipped to undertake it, and to close down the less efficient plants. By operating the surviving plants at full capacity, it is hoped to secure economies and reduce costs and prices. How far this will in fact happen must depend upon the circumstances of each industry. If the capital both of the enlarged and of the closed down firm is already in existence, an economy from a fuller utilisation of existing machinery is not relevant. (It is, of course, true that the receipts of the enlarged firm will be increased.) The economy must arise, if it arises at all, from an increase in the efficiency of the utilisation of labour or of raw material when a firm is working at full capacity, as compared with that when it is working below its best capacity. In some industries, in steel manufacture for example, such economies are probably to be found. The economy may arise alternatively from an introduction of new equipment which is profitable when the firm is fully occupied, but would be unprofitable if the firm were only so much occupied as it would have been apart from the enforced concentration of production.

§ 2. The Coercion of the Consumer. It is important to observe that these arguments for a measure of interference have their origin in the foibles of the consumer. It was necessary, we saw, to interfere on occasion to secure combination because there existed economies of combination but not economies of expansion. This can occur only where there is a cost of persuading customers to move their custom. It was necessary to interfere to secure concentration of production in the best equipped works because the free play of forces did not bring this about; but we have seen in an earlier chapter that if there were perfect competition, a contraction of output, which might be made necessary by a decline in demand, would take the form of the complete closing down of the least efficient producers and the concentration of production in the hands of the most efficient. Interference is only necessary to secure this end if competition is not perfect. Rationalisation is often, in fact, a cure, not for an excess of competition, but for a deficiency of it.

If the consumer is to be made the scapegoat, we must study the reasons for his delinquencies. He may attach himself to a single producer, and refuse to transfer his custom to another, who offers the same product just a little cheaper, for either of two reasons. There may be a genuine economy to him in buying from this particular producer, because he is nearer, and the freight on the goods concerned is less, or because, as may happen in the case of a shop, the saving to be obtained from going to the alternative shop is less than the value of the time, or fare, or petrol, spent in going there. Sometimes a nearer producer or a nearer agent can be relied upon for better service, or for quicker spare parts, than would be obtained from another. Sometimes the fact that he is buying some things from that producer makes it more economical to buy others as well. In all these cases, there is an adequate economic justification for the preference shown by the consumer, and his custom can only be transferred to a less convenient producer or shop at a loss to himself. A compulsory transfer would only increase welfare in these circumstances if the economies secured by concentration of production more than offset the extra costs and inconveniences of the consumers.

But consumers attach themselves also to individual producers for far less admirable reasons. There is an economy of effort, it is true, if I can immediately respond to the stimulus of an empty cigarette case with the thought 'Gold Flake from Jones's.' But, once I have learned a new reaction, it is no harder for me to respond 'Players from Smith's.' It may take thousands of acres of paper, or a prolonged and considerable difference of price, to penetrate my consciousness and teach the old parrot a new cry. But once I have learned it, I am as likely to be better off as worse.

It is possible, then, that by compulsorily combining firms

and limiting the varieties of products turned out, we may succeed in bringing firms, which are prevented from growing by the cost of attracting customers from equivalent substitutes, to a size nearer to the optimum size apart from considerations of such sales costs.   By doing this, we may make the commodity cheaper and increase the welfare of the consumers of both the previously independent varieties.   To the question how far we should bully the consumer, there will always be two answers.   There are some for whom variety is the salt of life, who would feel themselves genuinely aggrieved if they thought that anything were done to reduce the present opportunities of discovering the perfectly satisfactory object, to restrict the freedom of the craftsman on the one side, the purchaser on the other, to express his individual taste in the design or choice of goods.   There are others who are perhaps no less sensitive to their surroundings, but more willing to follow the common taste.   Their carpets, their curtains, their pictures are all of a design which local fashion has decreed.   They have to some extent standardised themselves. For the minority individuality is essential, for the majority cheapness is willingly bought at the cost of conformity.   If Mary and Martha can both be persuaded that they prefer the same size and shape of bed, they will both get it cheaper than if they are persuaded by expensive advertisements, for which they must ultimately pay, that they like different shapes.   So long as profits can be made by supplying odd sizes, the manufacturer will do so.

Attempts have therefore been made to limit the possible variety.   In the United States, for example, there was established in 1922 a Division of Simplified Practice of the Department of Commerce.   The varieties of sizes and dimensions of everyday commodities have been diminished, and production has been concentrated on a reasonable number of different types of each commodity.   Before standardisation, about 80 per cent of production was of about 20 per cent of the varieties.   The remaining 80 per cent of varieties were responsible for only 20 per cent of the sales.   Instead of

4,460 types of shovels, spades and scoops, for instance, some 384 remained in production, enough even then to provide the perfect shovel for every purpose. Before 1922 a hospital patient might have been accommodated in a bed of any of 33 lengths, 34 widths, and 44 heights. From that date President Hoover, a more kindly Procrustes, fitted him to one bed of standard length, width, and height.

In this country simplified practice has as yet made rather less headway, despite its apparent success in other countries. In war-time, however, and to some extent since the war a serious attempt has been made in some industries to establish standards and reduce varieties. We have, however, on the whole preferred our freedom. We are free to go into any shop we wish, and to ask for anything that we wish across the counter. We are free to ring up the butcher or the baker or the grocer, to tell him to send us immediately anything we please. We are free to go into a hatter's or a shoemaker's and to select the particular hat or the particular pair of shoes that catches our fancy. Despite this, in normal times, the controllers of industry manage to put the right men into the right places with some 95 per cent of accuracy. But they do it not by giving us what we want, but by making us want what they can give us. It is as well to remember just occasionally what we pay for our freedom. We spend something over £200 millions a year on advertisement. There are, as we have seen, many commodities of which the total distribution costs represent more than 40 per cent of the final price; there are not a few of which they amount to just about a half. Of these costs, some part, the handling and transporting costs, are unavoidable in any circumstances, but a large part is the cost of persuading us to be reasonable in our demands and of carrying the slow-moving stocks consequent upon our unreasonableness. We might sometimes have both the alternatives that are open to us for little more than the price we pay for our freedom; we might have, perhaps, both beef and mutton for little more than the cost of the organisation necessary to allow us the choice. Most of us would abhor rations, but we must remember the price that we pay for our abhorrence. The armed forces can buy coal, meat, clothing at a fraction of the price that the civilian population must pay for these things. Nor is the loss limited to the cost of persuading us. In many industries all the firms, big as well as small, could produce more efficiently were they assured of a large and certain market. It is, as Adam Smith told us, the extent of the market that limits the division of labour, and it is you and I who determine the extent of the market. It was, we all know, 'the rolling English drunkard made the rolling English road.' It is the contrary English customer who has done most to make the contrary English firm.

§ 3. Intervention to Mitigate the Severity of Competition. So long as rationalisation is concerned with the elimination of frictions, with building an industrial structure closer to that which a perfect competition would establish, we can have little cause for doubt or suspicion. But rationalisation, as it was conceived and applied in the 1930s, had an additional object which we must now examine. Its purpose was so to alter the supply either of the equipment available for production, or of the product itself, that the losses of the manufacturer might be reduced, or his profit increased. Now this is not *prima facie* objectionable. An industry which produces too much is, we have seen, fined until it contracts its output. Profits, and wages also, if the manufacturer attempts to pass on his losses, will be reduced below their normal level until capital and labour have been discouraged from entering that industry for sufficiently long to restore an equilibrium between the capacity of the industry and the demand for its products. If an industry is to be fined for no other reason than that it may adjust its capacity to demand, why should it not quickly make the adjustment and reduce the duration of the fine? Rationalisation thus becomes the substitution of anæsthetic surgery for industrial gangrene.

To this plea, two answers can properly be made. First it may be said that once society has used resources to construct

equipment for a certain industry, it has an advantage in employing all that equipment during its whole normal life.   To
destroy equipment is both wasteful and wicked.   To this the
shipbuilding shareholders (in the 1930s shipbuilding was one of
the industries believed to have a long-term excess of capacity)
may not unreasonably reply, 'It was we who provided the
capital.   We erred in providing too much.   Why should we receive for years less than we should have received, had we spent
less on providing you with capital, more on riotous living?   If
we had given you too little capital, you would have expected us
quickly to increase it; if we give you too much, why should we
not as quickly decrease it?'   So long as capital is provided
by private individuals, I find this plea difficult to answer.
It is, however, far less convincing when the error of forecast
has led not only to an excess of capital, but also to an excess
of labour, which without rationalisation of this kind might find
useful employment at somewhat lower wages and with somewhat lower profits in the industry to which it is trained, but
with a scheme of rationalisation must be wholly unemployed.

Secondly, it may be said that the power so to adjust
capacity to demand that a condition of normal profits is
quickly restored, cannot exist apart from a further power to
alter capacity in such a way that more than normal profits
can be earned; that in fact industries will be likely, where there
are errors of over-investment, to attempt to obtain normal
profits not only upon the desirable investment, but also upon
the superfluous investment.   The whole problem of how far
and in what circumstances a monopoly is able to increase
the stability of industry, and how far our powers of controlling
monopolies are sufficient to justify us in entrusting to them
opportunities which are open to misuse, is too wide to be
discussed here.   Its treatment must be left to another volume
in this series.

Where an industry is declining permanently, as the cotton
industry has been doing, or where modernisation of equipment is dependent upon the concentration of output in a
smaller number of plants, there is sometimes a good case for

semi-compulsory amalgamation of this kind. But a large proportion of the so-called 'rationalisation schemes' of the 1930s represented a misguided attempt to exorcise depression by adjusting capacity to the low level of requirements of the bottom of the depression. Compulsory and state-subsidised destruction of valuable equipment in potentially growing industries is the least appropriate measure yet discovered for curing a depression.

§ **4. Competition or Control?** There is, I think, a more fundamental criticism of this type of intervention. It is in effect a means of softening the blows with which our economic system punishes errors in the distribution of resources. We have moved now very far from the days of *laissez-faire*. Wages are seldom, if ever allowed to find their natural level. Unemployed men may not now be starved into accepting jobs. It is but a slight step forward to say that mistakes of over-investment should be punished as lightly as is possible. But we must remember that it is by a system not only of rewards but also of penalties that a competitive economic system works. If errors are to go unpunished, or right judgments to receive no higher reward than wrong judgments, the forces making for perfect adjustment may be so weakened as to become inoperative. We are to-day attempting to work an economic system in which we pay lip-service to competition, but at every turn mitigate or prevent the working of those sanctions on which a perfectly working system of competition depends. It may be that this compromise is an impossible one, that we can afford no longer to stick pins into the clockwork and expect it to go.

This is not an easy argument to dispute. What will or will not contribute in the end to the smoothest running of the economy is very much a matter of judgment. I should myself want also to emphasise the uncertainties and risks of the economic system and the danger that, with the increasing specificity of much investment with modern techniques, entrepreneurs may be less willing than is desirable to invest as much as is needed in a ruthlessly competitive economic system in which the penalties of excessive investment are heavy and the rewards of insufficient investment are great. It has, for instance, been argued as a case for the nationalisation of the steel industry that a nationalised industry can carry an excess of capacity more easily than a fully competitive industry, and that it is very desirable that the steel industry, which provides the raw material of so much of our production and exports, should always err, if err it must, by having too much rather than too little capacity. But clearly such arguments concede the advantages of certain limited monopoly powers which can very easily be misused.

§ 5. The Importance of Scale.   May I end with a few words on the importance of scale? This book is primarily about the effects of scale. It would ill become the author to end by saying that scale is unimportant. I certainly do not believe that. On the other hand, I regard it as a sad consequence of the habit of drawing exaggeratedly steep two-dimensional cost curves, relating costs exclusively to quantities, that many economists tend to overrate the importance of scale and to underrate the importance of any other factors besides scale in determining costs. I do not myself believe that the immense differences between American production per head and British production per head in manufacturing industry are primarily the consequence of scale. It has been pointed out that American productivity bore much the same relation to British productivity when the American market was smaller than our own. I would explain the differences in terms rather of the tempo of work, of capital per head, of enterprise in the provision of capital, and of better organisation. Such explanations may be rather more wounding to our national vanities, but I believe they are nearer the truth.

If we are anxious to see the efficiency of British industry increased, I think we have to focus our attention on the intensity of competition, the vigour of entrepreneurs in eliminating and replacing obsolete methods and equipment, their determination to win markets by cutting costs and cutting profit margins as well as on the achievement of optimum scale.

But to say that these other things are also important will not, I hope, be held to imply that economic policy should not be directed when occasion requires towards the creation of market conditions in which businesses may be expected to seize to the fullest possible extent such economies—and they are often considerable—as truly derive from size. But surprisingly this is one of the fields in which the great advances of the past twenty years in the direction of making economics more quantitative has made least progress. Thanks to the Census of Production we now know much more than we did about the actual sizes of establishments or plants, though not as much as many of us would like about the size of firms —the units of central management and finance. We know also, thanks to recent researches, rather more about the extent to which production is concentrated in the few biggest concerns in various industries. But we know far less than we ought to know about the extent of the economies of scale. How much does a firm's cost of production increase if it is, say, 25 per cent below the optimum size? Is it a matter of 2–3 per cent? Is it a matter of 10 per cent? Are we, as consumers, wasting sixpence in the pound or five shillings in the pound by demanding variety? For which commodities may we with impunity be somewhat 'choosy'? For which ought we, if possible, to submit to standardisation? To these questions some of us would be prepared to guess the answers, and from time to time the estimates of industrialists come our way. But it would be greatly for the benefit both of policy-making and of clarity of economic thinking if more quantitative information were widely available.

MADE AND PRINTED IN GREAT BRITAIN BY WILLIAM CLOWES AND SONS, LIMITED
LONDON AND BECCLES